D1231509

A HISTORY OF
MODERN ENGLISH SOUNDS
AND MORPHOLOGY

BLACKWELL'S ENGLISH LANGUAGE SERIES

General Editor: Eric Dobson

A HISTORY OF
MODERN ENGLISH
SOUNDS AND
MORPHOLOGY

by Eilert Ekwall

translated and edited by
Alan Ward

OXFORD
BASIL BLACKWELL
1975

ISBN 0 631 14930 9

Translated from the 1965 edition of
*Historische neuenglische Laut- und
Formenlehre* (Walter de Gruyter
& Co., Berlin)

PRINTED IN GREAT BRITAIN BY
ADLARD AND SON LTD., BARTHOLOMEW PRESS, DORKING

CONTENTS

ACKNOWLEDGEMENTS

My thanks are due in particular to Professor E. J. Dobson for detailed criticism and many valuable suggestions, and to Mr Frank Whitford for helpful advice on problems of translation.

A. W.

TRANSLATOR'S INTRODUCTION

Eilert Ekwall's *Historische neuenglische Laut- und Formenlehre* was first published in 1914, and the fourth and last edition appeared in 1965, a few months after his death. In fact Ekwall never substantially revised the work, though the inclusion of recent major works on the subject in the Bibliography might suggest that he did. Can then a translation so late in time be justified? I think there can be no doubt about the answer. Interest in the history of English has recently been spreading well outside the small circle of specialists in the field, so there is clearly a place for an English version of this classic, whose clarity, learning, judgment, and remarkable inclusiveness within its small compass make it still unrivalled as an introduction to the history of modern English sounds and inflexions. It could only be improved upon by considerably increasing its length, and thus turning it into a different kind of book altogether.

However, much has happened in the sixty years since it was written. Not only has a great deal of scholarly work been done on the whole period, but since 1914 there have been substantial changes in British English in the matter of sounds and their distribution, in the positioning of stress in words, and even in morphology and syntax. Consequently, it seemed clear that something should be done to bring the work up to date, and so as not to obscure its distinctive quality and because of its own historical interest I have felt this was best done by means of detailed notes rather than by alteration of Ekwall's text or a lengthy introduction.

In the field of scholarship the most important events have been perhaps the following: the completion of the *New English Dictionary* and its corrected re-issue as the *Oxford English Dictionary* (OED); the appearance of Daniel Jones's *English Pronouncing Dictionary* (EPD) and the concept of Received Pronunciation (RP) expounded within it; the completion of Luick's *Historische Grammatik der englischen Sprache*; the appearance of the *Oxford Dictionary of English Etymology* (ODEE) by Onions, Friedrichsen and Burchfield; and Professor Dobson's massive work on *English Pronunciation 1500–1700*. Of considerable importance also has been the publication of Daniel Jones's *Outline of English Phonetics* and, more recently,

Professor Gimson's *Introduction to the Pronunciation of English*, and the work of the International Phonetic Association (IPA) whose system of phonetic transcription is now in general use. I have drawn attention in the notes to those matters in Ekwall's text which I have felt to be in need of correction or comment.

One or two points remain to be made. Ekwall's remarks on the language of poetry, though I have left them in the text, are now out of date, since for many years now there has been virtually no distinctively poetic or unpoetic pronunciation or vocabulary. The same may be said of 'archaisms' (except where these are used as direct or indirect quotations), and of stage-pronunciations except in the case of a very few of the older generation of actors. Likewise, in connection with Ekwall's comments on the subjunctive, it should be remembered that this mood is virtually dead in current English except in a few isolated expressions. As regards other aspects of usage, it is often difficult to give clear-cut information. Authorities frequently differ, and even in the case of RP not only does usage often vary within this type of English, but the whole status of RP has been changing during the past few years. Many non-RP pronunciations are nowadays heard in speech that is in a very real sense 'received' or 'accepted'. I have, however, preferred in the notes to quote for the most part from particular authorities to avoid the danger of relying overmuch on personal impression or unsupported evidence. Other comments on pronunciation will be found in the section on phonetic symbols.

As regards the translation, I have endeavoured to make this as close as was reasonably possible, though I have sometimes translated the same German word differently in different contexts for stylistic reasons provided there was no danger of ambiguity. Some words presented special problems: e.g. *Grundform*, for which there is no satisfactory single equivalent; *gebildet*, which I have rendered according to context as 'educated', 'polite', or 'refined'; and *auffällig*, translated as 'exceptional', 'remarkable', or 'unusual'. I have occasionally used the term 'half-stressed' for *nebentonig* to avoid such awkwardnesses as 'subsidiarily stressed' etc. I have in general kept very closely to Ekwall's text except in the following matters: a few printer's errors have been corrected; I have altered one or two phonetic symbols and terms (see 'Phonetic Symbols'); where Ekwall glosses an English word to identify it I have where necessary identified it differently, e.g. *sage* (§28) is glossed 'Salbei' (the G. word for the herb 'sage') by Ekwall; I have simply glossed as 'the herb'; I have altered NED to OED, Gill (the orthoepist) to the more correct Gil, and have rendered 'ne' ('neuenglisch') as 'ModE' rather than the now old-fashioned 'NE'. Finally, I have added to the Bibliography and made some alterations to the word-list: for details, see these sections. In my notes, 'first recorded' means 'first recorded by the OED'.

BIBLIOGRAPHY

Items added to Ekwall's bibliography are marked with an asterisk.

Baugh, *A History of the English Language*, New York, 2nd edn 1951.

Bloomfield, *Language*, London, new edn 1950.

Brunner, *Die englische Sprache*, Tübingen, 2nd edn 1960, 1962.

Danielsson, *John Hart's Works on English Orthography and Pronunciation*, Stockholm, 1955, 1963.

*Dobson, 'The Hymn to the Virgin', *Transactions of the Cymmrodorion Society*, Session 1954, pp. 70–124 (London, 1955).

*Dobson, *The Phonetic Writings of Robert Robinson* (E.E.T.S. 238), London, 1957.

Dobson, *English Pronunciation 1500–1700*, Oxford, 2nd edn 1968.

Dunstan, Kaluza, *Englische Phonetik* (Sammlung Göschen 601), Berlin and Leipzig, 1921.

Ellis, *On Early English Pronunciation*, London, 1869–89.

Franz, *Shakespeare-Grammatik*, Halle, 4th edn 1939.

*Fridén, *Studies in the English Verb from Chaucer to Shakespeare*, Uppsala, 1948.

*Gimson, *An Introduction to the Pronunciation of English*, London, 2nd edn 1970.

Horn, *Historische neuenglische Grammatik*, Strassburg, 1908.

Horn, Lehnert, *Laut und Leben*, Berlin, 1954.

Jespersen, *Lehrbuch der Phonetik*, Leipzig, 1939.

Jespersen, *Modern English Grammar I*, Heidelberg, 1909.

Jones, *English Phonetics*, Leipzig, 1949.

*Jones, *An Outline of English Phonetics*, Cambridge, 9th edn 1960.

*Jones, *English Pronouncing Dictionary*, London, 13th edn edited by Gimson 1967.

*Jordan, *Handbuch der mittelenglischen Grammatik*, Heidelberg, 2nd edn revised by Matthes 1934.

Kluge, *Geschichte der englischen Sprache*, Strassburg, 1901.

Kökeritz, *Shakespeare's Pronunciation*, New Haven, 1953.

*Long, *The English Strong Verb from Chaucer to Caxton*, Menasha, 1944.

Luick, *Historische Grammatik der englischen Sprache*, Leipzig, 1914–40.

*Mustanoja, *A Middle English Syntax, Part I*, Helsinki, 1960.

The Oxford Dictionary of English Etymology, Oxford, 1966.

The Oxford English Dictionary*, Oxford, 1888–1933. New Supplement 1972–.

Storm, *Englische Philologie*, Leipzig, 2nd edn 1896.

Sweet, *A History of English Sounds*, Oxford, 1888.

Sweet, *A New English Grammar*, Oxford, 1892, 1903.

Viëtor, *Elemente der Phonetik*, Leipzig, 6th edn 1915.

Viëtor, *Shakespeare's Pronunciation*, Marburg, 1908.

*Visser, *A Historical Syntax of the English Language*, Leiden, 1963–.

Western, *Englische Lautlehre*, Leipzig, 1912.

Wyld, *A History of Modern Colloquial English*, London, 3rd edn 1936.

Zachrisson, *The Pronunciation of English Vowels 1400–1700*, Gothenburg, 1913.

PHONETIC SYMBOLS

In the introductory section of his book Ekwall gives a list of the phonetic symbols he uses. They are for the most part those of the International Phonetic Association in use today, but the following points call for comment:

(1) I have brought Ekwall's system more into line with that of the IPA by using [θ] for [þ] (English *th* in *think*), and [ʌ] for [ɒ] (English *u* in *cut*). With regard to the latter it should, however, be noted that Ekwall describes this vowel as 'mid back', whereas in contemporary RP it is usually low central or low front.

(2) I have kept Ekwall's [a] for IPA [ɑ] to indicate G. *a* in *Mann* and (when long) English *a* in *father*, and [à] for IPA [a] as the 'low front' *a* in Fr. *madame*.

(3) I have likewise kept [ɪ] for English *i* in *sit*, [ò] for G. *o* in *Gott*, [ʊ] for English *u* in *full*, and [hw] for voiceless [ẉ] in the (now old-fashioned in RP) *wh* in *when*.

(4) I have also preserved Ekwall's distinction between the ' mid front' [è] in English *bed* and the 'low front' [ɛ] in English *there*. (Presumably Ekwall is here referring to the first element of the diphthong, [ɛə].)

(5) Ekwall uses [ɔ] for both English *o* in *not* and *au* in *laud*, describing both as rounded vowels. It should be noted, however, that in current RP the [ɔ] in *not* has only very slight lip-rounding, and that [ɔː] in *laud* has closer lip-rounding and is also a considerably higher vowel than [ɔ] in *not*.

(6) Ekwall notes that wherever there is no danger of misunderstanding he uses [e, o, i, u] instead of [è, ò, ɪ, ʊ].

(7) Diphthongs call for no comment except that I have kept Ekwall's [ou] for the diphthong in *no*, though in current RP the usual sound here is now [əʊ].

(8) Ekwall indicates ME (as well as OE) long vowels by a macron, e.g. $\bar{a}$, $\bar{\imath}$, and marks open $\bar{e}$ and $\bar{o}$ as $\bar{ẹ}$, $\bar{ọ}$, close as $\bar{ẹ}$, $\bar{ọ}$. These and other features of Ekwall's usage have been retained to avoid any possible misrepresentation of his system.

As regards terminology, I have substituted 'central' for the old term 'mixed' in the description of vowels like [ə], and have changed 'palatal(ized)' to 'front(ed)' etc. except where they would now be in accord with IPA usage.

I have used the IPA system in my own notes, though retaining [ɪ] and [ʊ] from Ekwall's system.

ABBREVIATIONS

AN	Anglo-Norman	ODEE	*Oxford Dictionary of English Etymology*
(Cent.) Fr.	(Central) French		
Du.	Dutch	OED	*Oxford English Dictionary*
(E)ModE	(Early) Modern English	O(N)F	Old (Norman) French
EPD	*English Pronouncing Dictionary*	ON	Old Norse
		PresE	Present English
(L)G	(Low) German	RP	Received Pronunciation (for definition see EPD)
(L)Lat.	(Late) Latin		
(E)ME	(Early) Middle English	WG	West Germanic
(L)OE	(Late) Old English	>	becomes (became)
		<	comes (came) from

Dobson: *English Pronunciation 1500–1700*: Vol. I quoted by page number, Vol. II quoted by paragraph.

INTRODUCTION

§1 The turn of the 16th century is usually chosen as the boundary between the ME and the ModE periods. A sharp distinction between the two periods cannot be made, of course, and a good case can be made out for a somewhat earlier as well as a rather later limit. The above date commends itself on several grounds. It is, for example, from the beginning of the 16th century that we have direct evidence of English pronunciation.

§2 The origins of a standard language go back to the 14th century. The existence of a literary language distinct from the dialects, based chiefly on the language of London, can be considered as generally recognized from about 1500. The unification first of all affected the written language. The colloquial language long continued to be dependent on the dialects, as direct evidence from the 16th and 17th centuries shows. Furthermore, various kinds of Standard English[1] can still be distinguished. We know, however, that already in the 16th century the English of the capital and its environs was taken as the standard.

In the present work only the standard language will be dealt with.

§3 As is well known, linguistic usage in the standard language of the south of England is still not entirely uniform, especially as regards pronunciation; see e.g. §§20, 75. Even wider and more numerous variations are certainly to be assumed for earlier ModE. Only by supposing different varieties of pronunciation within the standard language can variations like [i, e] and [ə] in *bird* etc., or the different development of *au* in *daughter* and *draught* etc. be explained. Variations in morphology are very marked, particularly in the case of strong verbs. Preterites such as *rid, begun*, and participles like *rid, broke, began*, which are not very common in EModE, become very frequent in the 17th and 18th centuries, only to become almost completely abandoned in the 19th century. In these cases variant forms must have been in use side by side throughout the period.

§4 Sources for the history of ModE sounds.

(a) Spellings are of limited value for the history of ModE sounds. Already in the 16th century the orthography was strongly dependent

---

[1] Ekwall uses the English expression here.

1

on tradition and no longer faithfully represented the pronunciation. Moreover, spelling according to the etymology became more and more the fashion in the EModE period; spellings like *debt*, *fault*, *habit* now appeared or became firmly established. However, 16th century spelling often remained pretty irregular and can therefore occasionally throw light on pronunciation. An important point is the beginning of the orthographic distinction between [i:] and [e:], [u:] and [o:]; cf. §§51, 76. In the following centuries the orthography became ever more regular, without being otherwise substantially changed. Pronunciation, however, has changed a great deal, and the difference between pronunciation and spelling has steadily increased.

(b) Rhymes are rightly regarded as a valuable source for the history of pronunciation. If a word whose pronunciation is unknown is found rhyming with a word whose pronunciation is known, it is possible to infer the pronunciation of the former. One supposition is, of course, that the rhyme is exact, and the value of rhyme as a criterion is obviously very closely bound up with the exactness of the rhyming technique. In the 16th century accurate rhyming was generally aimed at, and Shakespeare's rhymes for example are of no small value in establishing his pronunciation. Later poets, like Dryden, Pope, and others, work much more freely. A poet who, like Dryden, unhesitatingly rhymes e.g. *ale* and *ball*, *rain* and *wan*, gives us little certain information about pronunciation. Moreover, traditional rhymes are often used. For the later periods of ModE the rhyme-criterion is of restricted value.

(c) The evidence of grammarians. The most important help is given us by the direct observations on pronunciation to be found in the works of teachers of pronunciation, spelling-reformers, grammarians, and such-like. The earliest works of this kind spring mostly from the need for an improved orthography (Smith, Hart, Bullokar, Butler, Hodges and others) and make an attempt at a phonetic script. Often in these works attempts are made to describe the sounds, or the pronunciation is indicated by comparisons with foreign sounds. In other cases there are descriptions of English pronunciation intended for foreigners, or, less commonly, descriptions of foreign languages written for Englishmen, in which English sounds are compared with foreign ones. Somewhat later we find scholarly descriptions of English pronunciation (from Wallis, Cooper and others). Especially from the middle of the 17th century onwards there appeared numerous spelling-books, often provided with phonetic introductions (Price, Jones and others). In the 18th century a number of valuable pronouncing dictionaries were published.

The value of these works varies a lot. The qualifications of their authors were unequal. One would have a good ear and be able to detect delicate nuances of sound, another would be less talented in this respect. Many were more or less influenced by the written language, and thought they could hear distinctions in sound where there was only a distinction in spelling, or even considered the written form to be the standard for the pronunciation; others were less prejudiced. The observations of foreigners must be used with particular caution. Foreigners often had an imperfect knowledge of English and frequently interpreted sounds incorrectly or identified English sounds with quite different foreign ones. On the other hand they are mostly less conservative and freer from prejudice than the Englishmen. Their observations are often extremely valuable.

Since the observations of the grammarians are often unclear or ambiguous, opinions as to their interpretation frequently differ. It should be borne in mind that when observations seem to conflict with one another it is not necessary to conclude that one is right and the other wrong. Both may be right; the pronunciation may have varied.

On these works see Ellis, pp. 31–48, Horn, Lehnert, pp. 77–117, and especially Dobson, pp. 1–444. The following may be briefly mentioned here:

The *Hymn to the Holy Virgin* transcribed in Welsh orthography about 1500.[2] Palsgrave, *Lesclarcissement de la Langue Francoyse* 1530. Salesbury, *Dictionary* 1547; *Introduction* 1567. Smith, *De recta et emendata Linguae Anglicae scriptione* 1568. Hart, *Orthographie* 1569; *Methode* 1570. Bellot, *Le Maistre d'escole anglois* 1580. Bullokar, *Booke at Large* 1580; Aesop's *Fables* (phonetically transcribed) 1585. Mulcaster, *Elementarie* 1582. Gil, *Logonomia Anglica* 1619, 1621. Mason, *Grammaire Angloise* 1622. Butler, *English Grammar* 1633 f. Daines, *Orthoepia Anglicana* 1640. Hodges, *The English Primrose* 1644 (*Special Help to Orthographie* 1643). Wallis, *Grammatica Linguae Anglicanae* 1653. Price, *The Vocal Organ* 1665, *English Orthographie* 1668. Wilkins, *Essay* 1668. Miège, *Nouvelle Methode pour apprendre l'Anglois* 1685. Cooper, *Grammatica Linguae Anglicanae* 1685.[3] Jones, *Practical Phonography* 1701. Bysshe, *Dictionary of Rhymes*

[2] Professor E. J. Dobson, in his edition of the *Hymn* (1955), argues convincingly for a date earlier than 1500.

[3] Ekwall omits Cooper 1685 from his list; that this is a slip is shown by his frequent reference to Cooper in the main body of the work. An edition of the *Grammatica* in English which appeared in 1687 under the title of *The English*

1702. Lediard, *Grammatica Anglicana* 1725. Douglas, *Treatise on English Pronunciation* c. 1740. Elphinston, *Principles of English Grammar* 1765; *Inglish Orthoggraphy* 1790. Perry, *The Only Sure Guide to the English Tongue* 1776. Nares, *Elements of Orthoepy* 1784. Batchelor, *Orthoepical Analysis* 1809. Pronouncing dictionaries: Johnston 1764, Buchanan 1766, Kenrick 1773, Walker 1775 (*Rhyming Dictionary*), Sheridan 1780, Scott 1786, Walker 1791, Perry 1795, Jones 1798 (3rd edn), Smart 1836.

§5   Sources for ModE morphology.

For a study of morphology ModE literature, especially prose, offers the best material. In this field there is not so important a distinction between the literary and the colloquial language as there is in the case of spelling and pronunciation. At the same time the observations of grammarians† come into consideration; these often supply valuable information. The following account of the morphology, which only exceptionally takes note of the language of poetry, is based chiefly on a study of the prose literature. For the treatment of the strong verbs Price, *A History of Ablaut in the Strong Verbs from Caxton to the End of the Elizabethan Period*, Bonn 1910, has been valuable.

---

† (Ekwall's note) A summary of the observations of grammarians on the verb is given by Jacob Horn, *Das englische Verbum nach den Zeugnissen von Grammatikern des 17. und 18. Jahrhunderts*, Darmstadt 1911.

Teacher should also be mentioned here, since it differs in some details from the Latin edition.

The question of which, if any, other works should be added to Ekwall's list is bound to be arguable, but a strong case can be made for the phonetic writings of Robert Robinson (early 17th century; see the edition by E. J. Dobson, 1947), and for the *Writing Scholar's Companion* (1695) and *Right Spelling . . .* (1704), both of anonymous, though identical, authorship.

SOUNDS

I. STRESS

A. The Position of the Main Stress

GERMANIC WORDS

§6 In the case of Germanic words the rule has been from time immemorial that simple words and their derivatives are stressed on the root-syllable, but substantives and adjectives with prefixes are stressed on the prefix. Thus, e.g., *'foresight*, *'bygone*, but *for'bear*, *for'sooth*. Exceptions are mostly to be explained by analogy: e.g., *be'quest*, *under'standing* (sb.) after the verbs *be'queath* etc.; the verbs *'answer*, *'outlaw* after the sbs. Other exceptions are, e.g., sbs. and adjs. with the prefixes *mis-*, *un-*, like *mis'deed*, *un'truth*, *un'kind*; *al'mighty*, *e'leven*, *thir'teen*[1] etc. These stressings are in general attested from the EModE period onwards.

§7 Compounds as a rule have the stress on the first element (cf., however, §12 f.); so *'goldsmith*, *'landlord* etc. Exceptions are chiefly formations like *bill-of-'fare*, *man-of-'war*; place-names with an adjective as first element, like *Black'heath*, *South'ampton* (cf. also *New'foundland*, *North'umberland*); also, e.g., *all'hallows*, *north'west*; *back'gammon*, *man'kind*; pronouns like *my'self*, *who'ever*; adverbs and the like, such as *here'after*, *with'in* (see also §14).[2]

In poetry the stressing of the second element is common throughout the whole of the ModE period; cf. *eye'lid* (Shakespeare), *the wild sea'mew* (Byron). Formerly this stressing was probably more common in colloquial speech than it is today. The 18th century dictionaries

---

[1] EPD has: *'mis'deed*, less commonly *mis'deed*; level stress only for *untruth*; *un'kind*, less commonly *'un'kind*; *thirteen* has either (and normally) level stress, or may vary with sentence stress.

[2] EPD gives *'bill-of-'fare* (less commonly ,--'-); *'man-of-'war*; *'Black'heath* (most commonly, but may also vary with sentence stress); ,*Newfound'land* (the most usual, also the local, and English nautical stressing; -'-- is in use but less common); *All-Hallows* level stress only; *north-west* most commonly level, but may vary with sentence stress; *backgammon* also (less commonly) '-,--.

indicate it in widespread use. This marking of the stress may no doubt partly indicate level stressing (cf. §12); but it is scarcely possible to explain all cases in this way. Walker 1791 has, e.g., *black'guard, church'warden, sea'mew* (but *'seafight, -port,* and others); contemporaries have *hand'writing, post'chaise,* etc. Gil 1621 mentions variation in *churchyard.* Today *'churchyard,* but *Saint Paul's Church-'yard* (in Scottish *church'yard*); also *'church'yard.*[3]

ROMANCE WORDS

§8   Sbs. and adjs. which in French (Lat.) have only one syllable before the main stress mostly stress the first syllable, such as *'favour, 'probate, 'respite; 'foreign, 'modest.* In longer words the main stress in English is usually advanced to the syllable (which was normally countertonic) next but one before the tonic syllable;[4] endings like *-eous, -ial* count as two syllables. Regular are, e.g., *'accurate, ex'travagant, fa'miliar, 'inventory, 'testimony, va'riety.*

§9   These rules are often broken, however. The romance stressing has often been preserved, especially in later loanwords, such as those in *-ade, -eer (-ier), -esque, -ette, -oon:* e.g. *cha'rade, ca'reer, pictu'resque, ga'zette, bal'loon,* and in *fi'nance, la'pel, pe'tard, se'dan, au'gust;*[5] or *spect'ator, ho'rizon, i'dea* etc. Sometimes, however, early loanwords also have kept the romance stressing, like *af'fair, es'quire, ex'ample, de'vout, gran'tee,*[6] *les'see,* and others.

A heavy medial syllable has sometimes attracted the main stress, as in *ad'vantage, clan'destine, tri'umphal,* and words in *-ental, -entary,* like *funda'mental, ele'mentary* and the like.

The influence of related words explains, e.g., the following: *ad'vance, de'ceit, dis'tress, ac'quittance, con'dolence,*[7] *de'cisive, im-'postor, pro'fessor* (after verbs like *ad'vance, de'ceive* etc.), *'accuracy* (after *'accurate*), *'legislature* (after *'legislate*), *'spiritual* (after *'spirit*).

---

[3] EPD gives level stress as the rule in *churchyard,* but also (less commonly) *'--,* as well as variation according to sentence stress. The surname is always stressed *'--.*

[4] In order to make Ekwall's point clearer I have added the words 'in English', and used the technical terms of Romance philology: *tonic* refers to the syllable that bore the main stress in Latin and/or French, *countertonic* refers to a half-stressed syllable.

[5] EPD also (less commonly) *'--* in *finance. August* (the month and proper name) is stressed *'--;* Ekwall here means the adjective.

[6] *grantee* is not a particularly early loanword, being first recorded in 1491.

[7] EPD also (less commonly) *'---.*

§10 In earlier ModE different stressings from those current today are often attested.

The romance stressing is often retained. In the 16th century (and to some extent later) the following, e.g., were stressed on the final syllable: *aspect, colleague, import, outrage, purlieu*; and in the 18th century, e.g., *carat, frontier, memoir, ridicule.* Walker 1791 stresses *car'mine, pre'text, commo'dore, reser'voir, pla'card.* All these are now stressed on the first syllable. Often the stress still varies, as in *access, courtesan, survey*, and especially in late loan-words like *debris, éclat, gourmand, levee.*[8]

The so-to-speak 'regular' stressing is sometimes kept in earlier ModE where the PresE stress is due to analogical influences. Thus the first syllable used to be stressed in *acceptable, confessor* (down to the 19th century), *concordance* (still *c.* 1800), *corrosive, decretal, surveyor* (today *ac'ceptable* etc. after *ac'cept* etc.); and the middle syllable of *cavalry, infantry* (today *'cavalry* etc., perhaps through contrast-stressing). On the other hand, the regular stressing has sometimes survived to the present day, while in earlier ModE irregular stressing occurred. Thus previously *blasphemous, mischievous, retinue*, were stressed on the medial syllable (after *blas-'pheme, mis'chieve* (vb), *re'tain*); today *'blasphemous* etc. *Accessary, anchovy, consistory, decadence, interstice, pianist,* and others still vary (*'accessary* or *ac'cessary* etc.).[9]

§11 Verbs with prefixes are stressed, on the model of Germanic verbs like *beseech, overlook*, mostly on the stem syllable: e.g. *de'ny, pro'ceed, a'bandon, counter'mand.* Exceptions are explained by the influence of related words, e.g. *'combat, 'promise, 'conjure* (after *'combat* (sb.), *'promise* (sb.), *'conjurer*) etc., *'consummate, 'prosecute* (after *'consum'mation* etc.) and similar cases, or as due to sound-laws (cf. §8) as in the case of *in'terpolate, in'terrogate* etc., or by the retention of foreign stressings, like *acqui'esce, perse'vere* (after Lat. -'*esco*, *perse'vero*).

The expected stressing is not infrequently retained in earlier

---

[8] EPD has only *'access*, *,courte'san*, the vb *survey* only -'-, the noun *'survey* and (less commonly) *sur'vey*; *debris, eclat, gourmet* all stressed only on the first syllable, *levee* 'royal reception' only on the first, in the sense 'embankment' mainly on the first, but also (less commonly) on the second.

[9] EPD only -'--- in *accessary*; mainly '--- but (less commonly) -'-- in *anchovy*; only -'--- in *consistory*; mainly '--- in *decadence* but also (less commonly) -'--; only -'-- in *interstice*; mainly '--- in *pianist* but also (less commonly) -'--.

ModE, while the present-day one is the result of analogical recon-
struction. Thus *'ambush, 'envy, 'exile, 'traverse*[10] were formerly often
end-stressed. Words like *'confiscate, 'consummate,*[11] *'contemplate*
mostly had the stress on the middle syllable up to the 19th century.
Persevere is stressed *per'sever* by Shakespeare.

B. Level Stress

§12   In many words today two syllables are spoken with strong
stress. How old this stressing is is uncertain. It is fairly clearly
mentioned by Elphinston 1765 (in *gold-watch, sea-side,* and similar
cases). Walker 1791 gives *amen* as the only word 'which is pronounced with two accents when alone'; evidently he meant 'the only
uncompounded word', since in 18th century dictionaries (Sheridan
1780, Scott 1786, Walker 1791, etc.) two syllables were frequently
marked with strong stresses in compounds. The statements of the
authorities often contradict one another, however; thus end-stress
is frequently given as well as level stress. Probably level stress had
already developed, but the orthoepists had not yet clearly realized
this.[12] Walker 1791 has, e.g., *'bay'window, 'by-'end, 'by-'law, 'fuller's
'earth*. In the case of adjectives he mostly marked the first or second
element with strong stress: so, e.g., *'hard-favoured, 'highminded;
clear'sighted, high-'spirited*; but he also has, e.g., *'high-'coloured,
'high-'heaped*. In the 1806 edition the number of words with two
accents is greater; examples are *'game'cock, 'penny-'wise, 'water-
'gruel*.

§13   Today, level stress is found chiefly in compounds, especially
in formations of a more or less incidental kind where the first
element can be regarded as an attributive. Here belong, e.g., substantives in which the first element indicates the material (as in
'gold 'watch, 'plum 'pudding, 'tin 'soldiers), or is in apposition (as in
'Prince 'Consort, 'tom 'cat, 'twin 'brother), or is an adjective (as in
'common'sense, 'easy 'chair, 'high 'road,[13] *'roast'beef*), or in individual
cases such as *'penny 'stamp, 'evening 'dress, 'parish 'church, 'country
'doctor, 'India 'rubber, 'sponge-'cake*, or place-names like *'Hyde 'Park,*

---

[10] EPD also has (less commonly) *tra've̦rse*.
[11] Ekwall here means the verb; the adjective is stressed –'--.
[12] Level stress must be much older than the later 18th century: see Dobson, §3.
[13] EPD only *'high-road*.

'Cheap'side, 'Graves'end, 'Guild'hall;[14] adjectives like *'dark 'eyed, 'good-'looking, 'ready-'made, 'red-'hot;*[15] adverbs like *'down'hill, 'in'side,*[16] *'mid'stream,* etc.

Also derivatives with prefixes whose meaning is strongly underlined often have level stress, such as *'un'kind, 'un'do, 'arch'bishop, 'ex-'manager, 'sub-'editor,* and so on. Level stress occurs in other words too, e.g. in interjections like *'a'men, 'hal'lo, 'hur'rah;* in foreign proper names like *'Ber'lin, 'Chi'nese, 'Water'loo;* in *'thir'teen, 'four'teen* etc. In all these cases a pronunciation with a strong subsidiary stress on the first syllable is also common; indeed, the initial stress has developed from this subsidiary stress.

C. Rhythmic Stress

§14 The English language has a marked liking for rhythmical movement, that is to say, for regular alternation of strongly and weakly stressed syllables. This tendency often causes changes in stress.

In EModE, words like *com'plete, su'preme, for'lorn, un'backed* were stressed on the first syllable when followed by a noun with initial main stress. Shakespeare has, e.g., *'complete 'armour, 'distinct 'offices, 'supreme 'fair,* and the like. Similar cases are also to be found later, though less frequently. Walker mentions e.g. *'commodore 'Anson* as against *commo'dore.* Today examples such as *'Berlin 'wool, 'thirteen 'men* belong in this category, though they may also belong in the following one.[17] In words with level stress the strength of the stress on the first element is often diminished when following a syllable with main stress, and that on the second element likewise when preceding such a syllable. Examples are: the *'old arch'bishop, he is 'so good-'natured; 'afternoon 'tea, 'straw-hat 'factory,*[18] and the like.

The stressing of certain adverbs, prepositions, and similar words

[14] EPD also (less commonly) *'Cheapside, Graves'end, 'Guildhall* (esp. when attributive).

[15] EPD gives *good-looking, red-hot* as also varying with sentence stress; *ready-made* as *'---* when attributive.

[16] EPD gives *downhill, inside* as also varying according to sentence stress.

[17] Cf. also EPD observations on sentence stress above.

[18] Insofar as the locution can be said to exist, its stressing would now be *'straw'hat 'factory.* EPD does not give *straw-hat* (though these are still worn).

also varied in EModE, to some extent undoubtedly for rhythmical reasons. Examples are *among, within, without, forthwith, henceforth, sometime.* Cf., e.g., *I've 'cursed them 'without 'cause* (Shakespeare). Variation is frequently attested in the 18th century, and still occurs in prepositions (*until, within,* etc.).

II. THE VOWELS

A. Vowels in Stressed Syllables

QUANTITY

Shortening before a single final consonant

§15 This phenomenon occurs chiefly in the period following the loss of unstressed *-e*, i.e. in the late ME and EModE periods. That the shortening was fairly late is indicated by the fact that ME $\bar{\imath}$ and $\bar{u}$ were rarely shortened; the reason for this is evidently the diph-thongization of these vowels that took place in the 15th century. That the shortening took place partly in the EModE period is proved by the result of this change in words like *good* [gud]; the shortening in this case must have occurred after the change of [u] to [ʌ], i.e., after about 1600.

The shortening is widely attested by the earliest grammarians. Spellings indicating shortening are frequent in the 16th century and earlier.

Simultaneously with the vowel-shortening there occurred lengthening of the final consonant.

§16 *Examples.*

ā mostly remained long except before [ð, þ] as in *Bath, swath* (< ME *Bāþe, swāþe*;[19] on PresE [aː] cf. §46), and in the often weakly-stressed *are, have* (§§273, 278).

ai is (exceptionally) shortened in *again* [e, ei], probably influenced by *against,* and in *said, says* [e], probably through lack of stress.

---

[19] But there was an OE *swæþ*, ME *swaþ* which could account for the short vowel in EModE. It should be noted also that the pronunciation of the place-name *Bath* < OE *baþum* has clearly been influenced, in both vowel and final consonant, by the analogy of the common noun *bath* < OE *bæþ*.

ę̄ > [e] especially before [d, t], as in *bread, dead, head, red; fret, sweat, threat*; also, e.g., in *death, deaf.* But [iː] in *knead, lead* (vb), *heat, heath,* and others.

ẹ̄ is sometimes shortened to [i], as in *hip* (the berry), *rick* 'hayrick', *sick, sprit,* EModE *thrid* for *thread* (< ME *þrēd*). For the most part the long vowel has been retained, as in *breed, heed, cheek, reek, green.*

ǭ: shortening in, e.g., *got, hot, wot* 'know', *trod* (perhaps after *trodden*); *cloth, froth; anon, gone, shone.* But usually the long vowel has been retained, as in *load, road, boat, oath. Sloth* varies between [ɔ] and [ou].[20]

ọ̄ (EModE [uː]). Early shortening gave [u], whence [ʌ] as in *blood, flood, stud* 'mare';[21] *done; glove;* later shortening gave [u] which remained unchanged, as in *good, stood; foot, soot; book, brook.* The long vowel has been retained in *food, mood, shoot, loom, moon* and others.

In the 17th and 18th centuries [ʌ] is often attested in words which now have [u], and vice-versa; *soot* still varies between [u] and [ʌ].

For ME *ū*, cf. §103.

[ɔː] from ME *au* is sometimes shortened in *because* (biˈkɔːz, -kɔz]. In EModE a long vowel is often attested in words which today have a short one. Thus Hart 1569 and Butler 1633 give a long vowel in *death,* Bullokar 1580 in *fret, tread*; Gil 1621 in *threat,* Cooper 1685 in *sweat.* Ben Jonson writes *hote* instead of *hot* 'hot'. ME *ǭ* appears as [uː] in Hart 1569 and Bullokar 1580 in, e.g., *book, took,* in Gil 1621, e.g., in *foot, brook,* and still, apparently, in *book* in Cooper 1685.

Long vowels before consonant-groups

§17 The OE long vowels before lengthening groups such as *ld, mb, nd, r* +cons.,[22] insofar as they were not shortened in ME (which was, e.g., the case with all vowels before *ng,* as in *long* < OE *lāng,* and with *ǭ,* and for the most part *ē* before *nd,* as in *bond* < OE *bānd*)

---

[20] Now only [slouθ].

[21] Ekwall 'Stute', but there is some misunderstanding here. The meaning 'mare' for *stud* is given by the OED as confined to Scotland, rare, and obsolete. The usual meaning is 'an establishment where horses and mares are kept for breeding'.

[22] This is not strictly correct; the lengthening occurred before *r* +certain voiced consonants.

were mostly preserved. Examples: *cold, field, child, bind, found, climb, comb*. Before *r*-groups ME *ǭ, ū* have mostly been preserved as long vowels, EModE [uː], PresE [ɔː], as in *board, hoard, forth, mourn*; a short vowel, however, in *word*, EModE [wurd], whence [wəːd]. A long vowel has been retained in *fourth, fourteen*, with EModE [oːu]; *forty*, on the other hand, had [ɔ] in EModE,[23] whence through later lengthening [ɔː]. In words like *earth, learn, beard, earn* the pronunciation varied much in earlier ModE between long and short; for details cf. §57.

In some cases a PresE short vowel contrasts with an EModE long as a result of the influence of related words. Thus *build, gild* [bild, gild] are due to *built, gilt* (with regular shortening), *friend* [frend], in earlier ModE long [friːnd], is due to *friendly, -ship* and the like, *wind* (sb.) [wind]—in poetry however still [waind][24]—to *windward* and the like.[25] *Gold* was still usually pronounced [guːld] (< OE *gōld*) c. 1800; PresE [gould], where [ou] corresponds to ME *ŏ* (cf. §88, 8), depends on the influence of *goldsmith* and the like. Cf. §21.

§18 Before *r*-groups vowels in French words were often long in ME and EModE; these long vowels have for the most part been retained; e.g. ME and EModE [uː] in *course, court* and the like, ME *ǭ* in *force, forge* etc. (where long vowels are attested in, e.g., Hart 1569, Gil 1621, Daines 1640; cf. further §79), ME *ā* in *scarce*. On the other hand ME *ę̄* before *r*-groups has been shortened, except in *pierce*; on these words, as on *fierce* etc. with ME *ę̄*, compare §§52, 57.

§19 Before [ʧ] long vowels have mostly been preserved, as in *each, preach, coach, pouch*. Shortening has occurred in *ditch, rich* and the like (with ME *ī*), in *breeches* [briʧiz] with ME *ę̄*, EModE [iː],[26] and in *touch* (ME *ū*).

§20 Fairly late, but in the 18th century at the latest, [ɔː] was shortened before *ls, lt*, as in *false, fault, salt*. Pronunciation still varies between [ɔː] and [ɔ].[27]

§21 In derivatives and compounds regular shortening (before consonant groups) often took place, while the simplex kept the long vowel. The regular quantitative sound-change has been preserved in,

[23] Usually, though not always.

[24] Hardly so nowadays, *pace* EPD; see the Introduction to the translation.

[25] The short vowel in *wind* is more likely to be due to *windy*.

[26] Dobson (§11) regards this as ME shortening of *ę̄ > i*.

[27] There is some evidence of shortening of *au* to *ŏ* in the 15th century; see Dobson, §29 and notes.

e.g., the following cases: *bonfire* [ɔ], *cleanly*,[28] *cleanse* [e], *Greenwich* [grinidʒ],[29] *husband, Monday, Southwark* [sʌðək], *vineyard* [vinjəd], compared with *bone, clean, green, house, moon, south, vine.* Cf. also cases like *Christmas* [krisməs] and *Christ, children* and *child.*

The shortening appears to be relatively late in *against* (with [e] in Hart 1569), *breakfast* (with [e] in Cooper 1685), *waistcoat* [weskət] (with [e] in Johnston 1764).

The long vowel has often been reintroduced or is making headway under the influence of the simplex. For example, beside [brekfəst, weskət], [breikfəst, weistkout][30] are heard. In the 18th century a short vowel is attested in, e.g., *cheerful* [e], *fearful* [e], *oatmeal, Shakespeare, therefore.*

Vowels in open syllables

§22 In words of Germanic origin ending in a suffix bearing subsidiary stress (such as *-y* < *-ig*) or ending in *-el, -en, -er* and the like, the quantity must frequently have varied in ME both where the stem vowel was short in OE and where it was long. In earlier ModE variation is still widely attested. Examples: *acorn, besom, even* (adj., adv.) (short in Bullokar 1585), *open; heaven, heavy* (long in both in Gil 1621), *nether, seven* (long in Hart 1569), all with a short vowel in OE; *errand* (long in Gil 1621), *herring, weapon* (long in Lediard 1725), *silly* (often *seely* in EModE), *other, mother; either, weary* (short in Price 1668), *holy, thousand* (both short in Bullokar 1580–), all with a long vowel in OE. On *father, rather* cf. §47, on *water* cf. §75. ModE shortening has perhaps taken place in *knowledge* [nɔlidʒ] (short in Hart 1569), *threepence, twopence* [θripəns, θrepəns, tʌpəns], both found with a short vowel since the 17th century.

§23 Variations in quantity also occur in words of French origin†. Thus in earlier ModE a long vowel is attested in *endeavour, measure, pleasant, pleasure* (e.g. in Gil 1621 and others); in PresE [e]. In words of this kind also ModE shortening perhaps took place;

---

[28] Now [e] only in the adj., [iː] in the adv.

[29] EPD also [gren-].

[30] EPD only [brek-]; [weiskəut] usual, also (less commonly) [-t-]; [weskət] old-fashioned.

† (Ekwall's note). The quantity of vowels in open syllables in Fr. and Lat. words presents very complicated problems; see esp. Luick (*Anglia* 30) and Jespersen (*M.E.G.* 4. 5 etc.). Since the quantity in such words remains on the whole unchanged in the ModE period an answer to these questions has not been attempted.

probably, e.g., in *faucet, laudanum,*[31] *sausage,* with [ɔ] < [ɔː] < [au], in *sausage* with [æ] < [æː],[32] and in *sugar* [ʃugə] with [ʃu] < [sjuː] since the 17th century.

Modern English lengthenings

§24   Examples belonging here will be dealt with under the respective vowels. On [aː] in *barn, last* etc., cf. §46; [ɔː] in *corn, frost,* cf. §75; [əː] in *herd, fir, turn,* cf. §§50, 68, 99.

QUALITY

a-sounds and *a*-diphthongs

a in *hat*

§25   Late ME *a* represents:†

1. OE (ON) *a*: OE *æ, ea*: e.g. *ass, hat, man, arm*; shortened *ǣ, ēa, ā*: e.g. *bladder, lather, lammas.*
2. OF (Lat.) *a*: e.g. *catch, art, card, cabin, manner*; AN *a* < *e, marvel, parson* etc.
3. OF *au* before a labial: e.g. *salmon, savage* (OF *saumon, sauvage*).
4. EME *e* before *r*: e.g. *carve* (OE *ceorfan*), *far, harbour, smart, tar, war* (OF *werre*); with *e* still written, e.g. in *clerk, Derby, sergeant*; with *ea, hearken, heart, hearth* (cf. §48).

§26   ME *a* has usually given PresE [æ]. Examples: *hat* [hæt], *man* [mæn], *salmon* [sæmən].

Late ME *a* was probably pronounced [a], and this pronunciation is to be assumed also for the 16th century.[33] French authorities (e.g. Bellot 1580) who compare the long vowel in *hate* with Fr. *e* (§29) equate short *a* with Fr. *a*. The stage [a] is to be assumed from the development to [ɔ] after *w* (§27); a distinction between the vowels in *man* and *wan* is never mentioned in the 16th century. The stage [æ]

[31] EPD only [ɔː] in *faucet*; [ɔː] subsidiary in *laudanum.*

[32] Only [ɔ] now in *sausage*: Ekwall is apparently referring to a 19th century vulgar form *sassage* recorded by OED. But see also §36 below.

† (Ekwall's note). The information about the origin of late ME sounds makes no claim to completeness. The intention is more to give lists of examples; in these the words are arranged according to the origins of the respective sounds. With regard to consonants such information has been considered unnecessary.

The examples are given in the current orthography.

[33] It is now thought that late ME *a* was a low front sound, i.e. Ekwall's [à] rather than [a].

is first unambiguously attested by Wallis 1653; as an intermediate stage between [a] and [æ], [à] (still current in northern English) is to be assumed. Somewhat later evidence for [æ] is that of Miège and Cooper 1685. No further development has taken place in the standard language.

No other pronunciation than [æ] is to be supposed for the standard language in the later modern period. When 18th century orthoepists (such as Nares 1784, Walker 1791) compare the English *a* in *hat* with Fr. or Italian *a*, these are inaccurate observations.

Note: Occasional [e] instead of [æ] in the older pronunciation of *catch*, *gather* depend on ME by-forms with *e*. *Any*, *many* with [e] derive from ME forms with *e*. The frequently recorded interchange between *then* and *than*, *wreck* and *wrack*, *yellow* and *yallow* in earlier ModE also derives from ME.

§27 After [w], [a] is rounded to [ɔ]. Examples: *wan* [wɔn], *wash* [wɔʃ], *quarrel* (kwɔrəl). The rounding failed, however, before [g, k, ŋ], and [a] here became [æ]. Examples: *wag* [wæg], *wax* [wæks], *twang* [twæŋ].

The rounding is first attested by Daines 1640, but to judge from spellings of *o* for *a* it had already occurred somewhat earlier.[34] The pronunciation [ɔ] is attested later by, e.g., Miège and Cooper 1685, Lediard 1725. The rounding of [a] to [ɔ] thus took place more or less at the same time as the fronting of [a] to [æ].

However, many authorities of the 17th and 18th centuries record the same vowel in words like *want* and *hat*, and poets of these periods unhesitatingly link words like *wan* and *man* in rhyme. Evidently two different developments of [a] after [w] are to be assumed, and in the earlier standard language forms like [wɔn, wɔʃ] appeared alongside [wæn, wæʃ] etc. Towards the end of the 18th century variation between [ɔ] and [æ] is still found in pronouncing dictionaries, e.g. in *quality*, *quantity*, *wan*. Since then [ɔ] has prevailed except in *swam*, which has [æ] after *began* (etc.), and in *quaff*, *waft* and the like, where *a* was often lengthened [kwɑːf, wɑːft];[35] [ɔ] also occurs, however, and is regular in *wasp*. On *warm*, *water* and the like, cf. §75.

On *a* in *pass*, *cart* and the like, cf. §46.

---

[34] It is in fact found already in Robinson's phonetic transcriptions *c.* 1617, though chiefly in unemphatic words (where it is invariable in *was(t)*). See Dobson, §194.

[35] EPD [kwɑːf], less commonly [kwɔf]; [wɑːft], less commonly [wɔft, wɔːft].

ā in *hate*

§28 Late ME *ā* represents:

1. OE (ON) *a*, *æ*, *ea* in open syllables: e.g. *bathe, hare, name, acre, hazel, ale, take*; rarely in closed syllables, as in *lady* (OE *hlæfdige*),[36] *waist* (ME *waast*).[37]
2. Frequently OF, Lat. *a*: e.g. *case, estate*; *able, table*; *age, rage*; *ache* (name of the letter *h*), *chaste, taste*; *scarce*; *bacon, parent*.
3. OF *au* before a labial or [dʒ]: e.g. *chafe* (cf. Fr. *chauffer*), *save, Ralph* (OF *Rauf*), *gauge* 'to measure' (Fr. *jauger*),[38] *sage* (the herb). On *change, chamber* and the like, cf. §§38 f.

§29 ME *ā* has become PresE [ei] except before *r*. Examples: *bathe* [beið], *hate* [heit], *taste* [teist], *gauge* [geidʒ].

The beginnings of the fronting of ME *ā*[39] are to be found in the 15th century. The difference between Fr. and English *a* had already struck 16th century orthoepists. The so-called Lambeth Fragment of 1528 (Ellis 815) mentions the similarity between English *a* and Fr. *e*, and the Frenchman du Guez in 1532 (Ellis 61) directs that Fr. *e* should be pronounced almost as broad as the English *a*. Evidently these authorities had the pronunciation of the letter *a* (i.e. ME *ā*) in mind. Later the English *a* in *hate* was frequently compared with Fr. *e* in *estre*, or the *ai* in *faire* (Bellot 1580 and others). The qualitative distinction between the *a* in *hat* and in *hate* was often mentioned, among Englishmen first by Butler 1633.[40] From these observations it follows that at least the stage [æː] had been reached *c.* 1500. This conclusion is confirmed by rhymes (*ā: ę̄* and the like) and spellings (*a* for *e* and vice-versa).[41]

The fronting was followed by raising. Towards the end of the 17th century half-open *e* [èː] is attested, as Cooper 1685 gives the vowels in *hate* and *set* as alike in quality. It is therefore theoretically probable that the intermediate stage [ɛː] had been reached round about 1600. In the 18th century [èː] became close [eː], and this was finally diphthongized to [ei], more exactly [eːi], about 1800. The pronunciation [ei] is mentioned by Batchelor 1809, Smart 1836, and others.

[36] So in late OE; earlier *hlǽfdige*.
[37] But note that both words had forms with open syllables in ME, the latter in disyllabic inflected forms.
[38] ONF *gauger*.
[39] It is likely that ME *ā* was a low front [aː], i.e. Ekwall's [àː].
[40] But see Robinson's evidence (Dobson, §101).
[41] But see Dobson, §100 n.

Strangely enough, up to about 1650 most English authorities (e.g. Palsgrave 1530, Salesbury 1547, Hart 1569, Gil 1621, Hodges 1644, Wallis 1653, and still Wilkins 1668) hold to the qualitative identity of the *a* in *hat* and the *a* in *hate*. This is particularly remarkable in the case of good observers like Hart, Hodges, Wallis and Wilkins. According to the view of some scholars two developments of ME *ā* are to be assumed: a popular, advanced one, in which *ā* was fronted earlier than *ǎ*, and a learned and courtly, more conservative one in which *ā* and *ǎ* developed parallel with each other. Probably, however, the observations, at least of the 17th century authorities, are not entirely accurate. Wallis, e.g., gives the vowels in *set* and *seat*, and in *will* and *meet* as identical in quality, which can hardly be entirely right. Likewise (and similarly with Hodges and Wilkins) he may have missed the difference between perhaps [æ] and [ɛː]. It should be noticed that as long as the vowel in *hate* remained at the [ɛː] stage there was no short vowel identical in quality with it; *e* in *set* was more close. In the 16th century a more conservative pronunciation [aː] or [àː] may have existed beside [æː].

§30 Before [r] or the [ə] developed from it ME *ā* has become PresE [ɛ(ə)]. Examples: *hare* [hɛə(r)], *chary* [tʃɛəri], *scarce* [skɛəs].

ME *ā* before [r] developed exactly the same as in other positions till towards the end of the 18th century. The first reliable observer of the distinction between the vowels of *care* and *hate* seems to be Perry 1795,[42] who uses different symbols for both. Evidently *ā* before [r] became [eː] and was later lowered to [ɛː].[43] Cf. the similar development of [oː] §78.

Beside [ɛə] there appears also [eiə] in words like *aeroplane* and the like. *Aerated* is usually [eiəreitid].[44]

ai in *nail*

§31 *ai* represents:

1. OE *æ, e, ǣ, ē+g, j*: e.g. *day* (OE *dæg*), *nail*; *way* (OE *weg*), *weigh*; *clay* (OE *clǣg*), *grey*; *hay* (OE *hēg*), *bewray*.
2. OE *e(a)* before [x]: e.g. *eight, neighbour*.[45]
3. ON *ei*: e.g. *aye, they*.
4. OF *ai*: e.g. *bailiff, jail, pay, vain*; and
   ei: e.g. *heir, feign, obey*.

Since the ME period the spelling has varied between *ai* (*ay*), and *ei* (*ey*). In pronunciation *ai* and *ei* had already fallen together *c.* 1400.[46]

---

[42] Noted a little earlier by foreign observers. See Luick, §588 and n. 2.
[43] For a different (and preferable) view see Dobson, §205 and n.
[44] EPD not [eiə] in *aeroplane*.
[45] *neighbour* has OE *ē(a)*.
[46] Earlier; see, e.g., Jordan, §95.

§32 ME *ai* fell together with ME *ā* in the 17th century[47] and has usually given [ei]; before [r], [ε(ə)]. Examples: *day* [dei], *eight* [eit]; *fair* [fεə(r)], *fairy* [fεəri].

In the 16th century the pronunciation of ME *ai* seems to have varied. Usually a diphthongal pronunciation is described. The first element of the diphthong is mostly analysed as an *a*, and this *a* was probably identical with the reflex of ME *ā* [æ:, ε:]. Such a diphthong is attested by Gil 1621. That a monophthongal pronunciation (*ai* = the reflex of ME *ā*) existed already in the 16th century is indicated by the fact that *ai* was often written for *a*, and vice-versa *a* for *ai*. The unhistorical spelling has established itself in, e.g., *mail* 'letter-post' (OF *male*), *vail* 'lower, let down' (Fr. *avaler*), *waist*. Less conclusive is the fact that French authorities (like Bellot 1580) compare the sound in *day* (like *a* in *hate*) with Fr. *e* in *estre* or Fr. *ai*, since the distinction between, say, [ε:i] and [ε:] would be easy to miss; or the fact that rhymes like *maid*:*persuade* were common in some poets, since these can be interpreted as rhymes between [ε:i] and [ε:].[48]

A diphthongal pronunciation is still attested in the 17th century by most English authorities (such as Hodges 1644, Wallis 1653, Wilkins 1668, Cooper 1685). Cooper, however, also mentions the monophthongal pronunciation; and this was, in fact, in his opinion the commoner. Towards the end of the century the falling together with the reflex of ME *ā* became general, and the later history of ME *ai* is the same as that of ME *ā*. Before *r* the falling together with ME *ā* seems to have taken place rather earlier than in other positions; Hodges 1644 gives *hair*, *pair* the same vowel as in *care*.

According to Jespersen (cf. *M.E.G.* 11. 4) [ei] in *day* goes straight back to EModE [ε:i] without an intermediate stage [e:]. He regards the falling together with ME *ā* in the 17th century as due to the diphthongization of the latter.

§33 In (*n*)*either*, *key*, *quay*, and in *Caius* (properly *Key's* or *Kay's*) *College* (Cambridge) ME *ai* has developed to [i:]:[49] [i:ðə, ki:, ki:z].

PresE [i:] goes back to EModE [e:]; ME *ai* in these words fell

---

[47] But rhymes and spellings show that this had already occurred in the 16th century, though probably in 'less careful' speech. See Dobson, §225, and cf. Ekwall tacitly below.

[48] Though this explanation is doubtful.

[49] [i:] in these words must derive from a ME variant with *ę̄*.

together with ME ẹ̄ under circumstances not fully understood. This pronunciation is attested by Hodges 1644 in *either*, *key*; spellings such as *eather*, *neather*, appear in the 16th century. The regular development from ME *ai* was still to be found in the 18th century. Thus Dryden rhymes *key* with *way*, Swift, and even Tennyson, *quay* with *day*. In Hart 1569 f. ME *ai* in *day*, *maid* etc. has fallen together with ME ẹ̄, and the reflex of ME ẹ̄ in other words beside *key* etc. is also attested in the 17th century. A parallel development of ME *ai* must be assumed here.

[iː] in *deceive*, *receipt* and the like, and in *raisin* (still with [iː] c. 1800) goes back to ME ẹ̄. Cf. also §51, 8.

§34 *Either*, *neither* are usually pronounced with [ai] today. This pronunciation or its ancestor is first attested by orthoepists from the second half of the 17th century;[50] the spelling *nither*, however, is according to the OED already found in the 16th century. The explanation of this pronunciation is uncertain.

PresE [ai] in *height*, *sleight* (instead of and alongside [ɛːi] in earlier ModE) is due to the influence of *high* and *sly*.

au in *law*

§35 Late ME *au* represents:

1. OE *aw*, *eaw*: e.g. *claw*, *raw*, *straw*, *sprawl*.
2. OE *af*: e.g. *auger* 'boring tool', *hawk*.
3. OE (ON) *ag*: e.g. *draw*, *maw*, *saw* (sb.); *awe*, *law*.
4. OE (ON) *a*, *æ*, *ea* before [x]: e.g. *laugh*, *taught*,[51] *slaughter*.
5. OF (AN) *au*: e.g. (<*al*) *haughty*, *jaundice*; *assault*, *falcon*, *fault* (on the *l*, cf. §128) etc.; (<*av*) *laundress*, *laundry* (cf. Fr. *lavandière*), *saunter* (from *s'aventurer*); (<Lat. *au*), e.g. *cause* etc.; (<*ao*), e.g. *brawn*, *flawn*,[52] *pawn* (piece in chess); (<nasalized *a* [ã], in part from earlier *e*), e.g. *pawn* 'pledge', *tawny*; *chamber*, *change*, *command*, *grant*, *haunt*, *sample* and the like (ME *chaumber* etc.).

In AN *au* was frequently written instead of *a* before a covered nasal, e.g. in such words as *chaumbre*, *chaunt*, *demaunder* (=Cent. Fr. *chambre*, *chant*, *demander*). This spelling points clearly to a pronunciation [au]. In

---

[50] First, apparently, in Jones 1701. On this, and on the explanation of the pronunciation, see Dobson, §129 n. 2. The *-i-* spellings are ambiguous.
[51] I.e. with late OE *ĕ* and *ă* for earlier *ǣ* and *ā*.
[52] I.e. 'flan'; *flawn* is no longer current.

ME the spelling in words of this kind fluctuated between *au* and *a*. It is not clear whether the only ME pronunciation was [au]—in which case the *a* would be attributable to the influence of Cent. Fr. orthography—or whether in ME two pronunciations, [au] and [a], alternated with each other. The spelling also varies between *au* and *a* in ModE. In certain positions, however, *a* occurs almost without exception, which perhaps points to [a] as the sole pronunciation in EModE. This is the case before *ng*, *nk*, as in *anguish*, *languish*, *flank*, *plank*, and also in an originally unstressed syllable, as in *ancestor*, *antler*, *brandish* etc. (There are, however, exceptions: cf. *ancient*, *danger*, etc., below).

6. Occasionally OF *ou*, *o*: e.g. in *vault* (sb.) (ME, OF *voute*), *vault* (vb) 'to spring' (Fr. *volter*).

7. EME *a* of whatever origin before -*ll* and *l*+cons.: e.g. *ball*, *fall*, *hall*, *salt* etc., late ME [baul] etc.

a remained, however, in words like *fallow*, *tallow* (with short *l*), in pet-names like *Hal*, *Sal* (for *Harry*, *Sarah*, *Sally* and the like), in the often unemphatic *shall* (but in EModE also [ʃaul] etc.), finally, often in late loan-words like *album*, *Alps*, *altitude*, *valve* and the like. Exceptional is *Alfred* [ælfrid].

§36   ME *au* has usually given PresE [ɔː]. Examples: *law* [lɔː], *hawk* [hɔːk], *ball* [bɔːl], *talk* [tɔːk].

The 16th century authorities still give a diphthongal pronunciation; thus Hart 1569 and Bullokar 1580. Hart compares *au* with German *au*, which points to [au]. As an intermediate stage between *au* and [ɔː] a diphthong [ɔu] or [ɔːu]—with rounding of the first element—is to be assumed. Such an [ɔːu] is still attested by Gil 1621 as existing in certain words alongside [ɔː]. Probably [ɔː] had already made its appearance towards the end of the 16th century in certain circles, as occasional spellings (*o* for *au*, or vice-versa) seem to suggest.

In the 17th century (and later) a monophthongal pronunciation is usually attested. Gil 1621 compares the sound in *tall*, *lawn* with German *a* in *Mahl*, *Haar*. Hodges 1644, Wallis 1653, Wilkins 1668, Cooper 1685 and others consider the vowel in *Paul* as the long equivalent of the short [ɔ] in *poll*. This monophthong was presumably the [ɔː] current today, which has thus remained unchanged since *c*. 1600.

From the fact that the monophthong is identified or compared with Fr. or German *a* by numerous orthoepists, some scholars have concluded either that PresE [ɔː] goes back first of all to [aː] < [au], or that in the earlier standard language [aː] existed as well as [ɔː] for older *au*. Traces of a change of [au] to [aː], whence [æː] and [aː], are indeed to be found. *Sauce* is given with [æː] by Johnston 1764 and Elphinston 1790, and [saːs] is still a vulgar pronunciation. The [æ] attested by Nares 1784 in *sausage* has evidently come from [æː]. The PresE pronunciation [tʃaːdrən] beside [tʃɔːdrən] for *chaldron*[53] can be explained by this change. But this [aː] or [æː] probably comes from dialects in which [au] regularly became [aː]. For the standard language, except in special positions, only [ɔː] is to be assumed. If the vowel in *hall* etc. is compared with Fr. or German *a* this is simply due to the fact that in 17th and 18th century English [ɔː] was the vowel closest in quality to the continental [aː]. It is to be noted that German *a* seems formerly to have often had a velar pronunciation, and that in Fr. there are two *a* sounds, a more fronted one [à], and a more velar one which rather resembles [ɔː]. In the earlier ModE period [ɔː] was often substituted for German or Fr. [aː] in loanwords. Examples are: *maulstick* < G. *Mahlstick*,[54] *gauze* [gɔːz] < Fr. *gaze*. Cf. also the older pronunciation [ɔː] in *eclat* (Nares 1784, Walker 1791, etc.), *spa* (< G. *Spa*;[55] [spɔː] Walker 1791; the spelling *Spaw* occurs already in Webster, *Duchess of Malfi, c.* 1610), *vase*[56] (still in Walker 1791). The ending *-oir*, as in *devoir, reservoir*, still varies between [wɔːə] and [waː].[57]

§37 Before labials and nasal groups ME *au* did not usually become [ɔː] but some kind of *a*-vowel. In most positions PresE [aː] has resulted; e.g. in *calf, command*; cf. §§44 f., where also divergent developments are dealt with. On *au* in *laugh* and the like, cf. §163. Before [mb, ndʒ] *au* has become [ei]; there are, however, exceptions. In *ancient, halfpenny* [ei] has resulted.

§38 Before [mb] ME *au* has given PresE [ei] in *Cambridge* (ME *Caum-, Cauntebrigge*, a Normanized form of OE *Grantanbrycg*) and *chamber* [keimbridʒ, tʃeimbə], whereas in *amber, ambsace, jamb* we have [æ]. The pronunciation of these words has varied greatly in the ModE period. The fore-runner of PresE [ei] in *Cambridge* is recorded by Gil 1621. Alongside it there appeared [au] and [a] in the 16th century, and [ɔː] and [æ] in the 17th. In the 18th century *chamber* was sometimes pronounced with [æ] and frequently with [æː, aː]. In words like *amber, ambsace, jamb*, spellings like *aumer, jaumbe*, attest the pronunciation [au] or [ɔː]; Walker 1791 mentions the pronunciation *aims-ace*. The relationship between the various pronunciations is unclear. [ei] is to be compared with [ei] in *save* and

---

[53] 'a measure of coal'; EPD gives only [ɔː].
[54] 'light stick used by painters'; ODEE derives from Dutch *maalstok*.
[55] Originally the name of a watering place in the province of Liège, Belgium.
[56] EPD still gives [ɔː] as 'old-fashioned' (alongside usual [ɑː]).
[57] *devoir* seems to be obsolete now. EPD gives [-waː], less commonly [wɔː] in *reservoir*.

the like (§28, 3); perhaps *au* had become *ā* already in late ME.[58] The
other variants are to be compared with similar variations in words
like *dance, grant.*

§39 Before [ndʒ] PresE has mostly [ei], even in an originally
unstressed syllable; examples: *angel* [eindʒəl], *change, danger* etc.
In earlier ModE a similar variation existed as before [mb]. The
ancestor of PresE [ei] is attested perhaps in Hart 1569, and certainly,
e.g., by Hodges 1644. Otherwise we find in the 16th century [au]
and [a], in the 17th century [a] or [æ], and in Butler 1633 the reflex of
ME *ai.* In the 18th century [æ] and [æː] are occasionally recorded,
e.g. in *angel, danger.* The relationship between these various pronunciations is unclear.[59] PresE [ei] here can be compared with the
[ei] in *gauge* (cf. §28, 3). Cf. also the variation in *chamber* and the
like (§38) and in *dance, grant* etc. (§45). *E'vangel, flange,* have [æ].

§40 Early information on *ancient,* PresE [einʃənt], is lacking.[60]
The ancestor of [ei] is given by Johnston 1764, Walker 1791 etc. The
pronunciation [æ] also existed in the 18th century. [ei] is from [au]
as in *change* etc.

§41 Of obscure origin is the pronunciation of *halfpenny* [heipəni].
Spellings like *hapeney* in the 16th century indicate perhaps that the
ancestor of PresE [ei] existed already in EModE. Perhaps cases like
save (< Fr. *sauver*) are comparable; in this case loss of *l* is to be
assumed already in late ME.[61]

a in *father*

§42 After the fronting of the long *ā* (§29) there was no long *a*
sound in English. In the 17th century, however, there appeared in
the standard language the sound which has developed into PresE
[aː]. This [aː] mainly derives from ModE *au* and *a,* as in *calf, calm;
cart, cask.*

The new sound is attested with certainty in the standard language
from the second half of the 17th century; earlier evidence is doubtful.

---

[58] *au > ā* in *save* etc. is dated *c.* 1300 by Jordan, §240. What Ekwall suggests as
a possibility here is now accepted as all but certain: see, e.g., Jordan, §224 (III),
Luick, §427, Dobson, §104.

[59] But see, e.g., Dobson, §104.

[60] This is not so: see Dobson, §62 (1) and §104. The ancestor of [ei] is given
already by Hodges 1644, and the reflex of ME *ă* already by Robinson.

[61] Ekwall's conjectures here are almost certainly correct. See Dobson, §§104,
239.

The first certain evidence appears to be in Price,[62] who in 1665 transcribes *half, salve* as *hafe, save,* and in 1668 gives '*a* small' (the same vowel as in *hallow, face*) in *balm, calm.* The testimony of Cooper 1685 is important: according to him the long equivalent of *a* in *man,* i.e. [æː], was used in *grant, barge* etc. Later the new long vowel is mentioned by many authorities.

§43   As regards the early evidence only Cooper's observation shows the exact sound-value. Price's evidence is inexact, but points rather to a front vowel than to PresE [aː]. In the 18th century foreigners in particular frequently confuse the sound with the reflex of ME *ā* [eː]; but even the Englishman Lediard 1725 transcribes the vowel in *face, name,* as *äh* as well as that in *aunt, daunt, draught, laugh.* A Portuguese grammar of 1731 rewrites *calf, half* as *quêf, hêf.* From these and similar observations it is evident that the new vowel, at least till about the middle of the 18th century, was usually a front one. We shall not go far wrong if we conclude from all these observations that the sound-value was [æː].

The pronunciation [æː] was still in use in the later half of the 18th century. Johnston 1764 and Elphinston 1765 equate in quality the long vowel in *cask* etc. and the short vowel in *cat* (the latter compares the *a* in *cat* with the short *e* of other languages). As late as 1809 the good observer Batchelor states that the *a* in *mat* differs only in quantity from the long vowel in *bard.* Ellis 1875 (*E.E.P.* 1148) testifies that at that time [æː] was often used in *calf, ask, bath* etc. This pronunciation is still current in America.

In 1875, however, [aː] was the usual pronunciation. The antiquity of this pronunciation is uncertain. Already in 1740 Douglas seems to indicate an *a*-vowel, though of uncertain quantity, in words like *chaff, chance, father* etc. The lexicographer Jones (in the 3rd edn, 1798) makes a qualitative distinction between the vowels in *father* and *hat,* the former being 'more open'. Perhaps [àː] is meant. In any case [aː] was the usual pronunciation in popular speech towards the end of the 18th century, and established itself also in the standard language in the first half of the 19th century.

§44   [aː] represents EModE [au] before (*l*)*f,* (*l*)*v,* (*l*)*m*: e.g. *calf, half; calve, halve; almond, alms, balm, calm, malmsey, palm, psalm.* The [l] was lost in the 16th century (on French words, however, cf. §128) and [au] came to stand before the labial. It is clear that the [aː] in these words is to be compared with the ME *ā* from *au* in *safe*

[62] Not certain evidence: see, e.g., Dobson, §104 (2) and n. 9.

(Fr. *sauf*) etc. (see §28, 3). In this case the [aː] would be explained as due to the loss of the second element of the diphthong. Since the monophthong remained separate from the *a* in *hate*, this loss must have taken place after the fronting of ME *ā*. Also the monophthongization must have occurred before the change of [au] to [ɔː]. Since the new sound is first recorded in the standard language after 1650, a parallel (dialectal?) development must have taken place, which displaced the regular one. The monophthongization probably gave first of all [aː], whence [æː] arose through fronting.

Till about 1650 our authorities (e.g. Bullokar 1580, Gil 1621, Hodges 1644) give the same diphthong or vowel [au, ɔː] in *calf*, *balm*, *calm*, etc., as in *talk*. Wallis 1653 still transcribes *half*, *calm*, etc., as *hauf*, *caum*, and there is even later evidence for [ɔː]. Sheridan 1780 mentions [ɔː] in *calm*, *psalm*, etc., as an Irish peculiarity. The [ɔː] attested in some words, like *halm*, *shalm*, since the 18th century could be a remnant of the old pronunciation; though the influence of the spelling can also be assumed. The latter is evidently the explanation of the [ɔː] in *almanack* and the like, and of [æl] beside [aː] in *almoner*, *psalmist*, *psalmody*, *salve*, and [æl] in *salvation*, *scalp*.⁶³ [ɔː] in *almighty*, *almost*, is due to the influence of *all*.

§45 [aː] represents EModE [au] before *-nce, -nch, -nd, -nt*: e.g. *chance*, *dance*; *haunch*, *launch*; *command*, *jaundice*, *slander*; *aunt*, *daunt*, *grant*;⁶⁴ before *mp* in *example*, *sample(r)*.

Earlier authorities (like Hart 1569, Bullokar 1580, Gil 1621, Butler 1633, Hodges 1644) give [a, æ] or [au, ɔː]. PresE [aː] and 17th and 18th century [æː] can clearly not have developed from [ɔː], and not from EModE [a, æ] either, since in this case we should have expected [aː] in words like *hand* and *stand* also. There remains the possibility that the sound comes from EModE [au], which would mean monophthongization of [au] to [aː] before nasal groups; this [aː] would then have given 17th century [æː]. The monophthongization would have been simultaneous with that before labials, and the monophthong would have entered the standard language at the same time as that in *half* etc. The difficulty is to explain the monophthong-

---

⁶³ EPD [ɔːl], less commonly [ɔl] in *almanack*; only [aː] in *psalmist*; [æl], less commonly [aː] in *psalmody*, but only [æl] in *salve*.

In some of these words *l* may never have been lost; also, learned words may have been influenced by Latin. See Dobson, §425 and n. 2.

⁶⁴ EPD has only [ɔː] in *haunch* and *daunt*, [ɔː] predominantly, but [aː] less commonly in *launch*, and [ɔː] usually, [aː] only 'rarely' in *jaundice*.

ization. Possibly it is to be interpreted as a kind of reduction[65] before the consonant group.

The old pronunciation [ɔː] was not altogether displaced, however. Cooper 1685 mentions [ɔː] beside [æː] in numerous words, such as *enhance, haunt, maunder, jaunt*. In the 18th century, orthoepists (such as Johnston 1764, Sheridan 1780, Walker 1791) frequently attest [ɔː] in certain words, especially *daunt, haunt, maundy, paunch, taunt, vaunt*, and [ɔː] is still common in various words. The influence of the spelling may partly explain this. It has evidently been due to the printed word that nowadays words like *launch* are often pronounced with [ɔː].[66]

The [æ] pronunciation has also survived. 18th century orthoepists (like Johnston 1764 and Walker 1791) frequently record it, but especially before *-nce, -nt*, as in *chance, dance, grant, plant*. It is not clear whether this [æ] derives from EModE [a] or is due to the influence of the spelling. It can be explained in part as a reaction against the pronunciation [aː] which began to make its way into educated speech towards the end of the 18th century. This [æ] is still to be heard. Other vowels also are occasionally evidenced in words of this sort, e.g. [à].

In late loanwords from Fr. various vowels are substituted for Fr. *ã*; e.g. [ɔ], as in *encore* [ɔŋ'kɔːə], *envelope* [ɔnvəloup, ɔŋ-], where Walker 1791 also has [ɔ]; or [æ], as in *gallant* [gə'lænt], *grand*, also in *artisan, partisan* (in all of which Walker 1791 has [æ]); or [aː] as in *avalanche, comman'dant*. *Jaunty* (Fr. *gentil*) has nowadays [ɔː] or [aː], according to Walker the *a* as in *father*, according to Sheridan 1780 [ɔː]. *Blancmange* has [aː, ɔ].[67]

§46 [aː] represents EModE [a] before final *f, s, θ, r*, and before *f, s, r*+cons.; e.g. *staff, class, bath, car, raft, bask, clasp, last, bark*. Here belong cases like *laugh, draught*; cf. §163. But [æ] is spoken in words like *chaffer, passage, barren; chaffinch*,[68] *passing*, etc., have conformed to *chaff, pass*.

[aː] (and 17th and 18th century [æː]) has arisen through lengthening. [æː] either goes back directly to [æ] or has developed from unattested older [aː] from EModE [a] (cf. §44). The lengthening is first recorded (in Cooper 1685) before θ, *sk, sp, st, r*+cons.[69] Before

---

[65] Ekwall 'Reduktion'.
[66] See §45 note 64.
[67] EPD usually [en-] in *envelope*; -'- 'rarely' in *gallant*; usually [æ] in *comman'-dant*; only [ɔː] in *jaunty*; usually [ɔ], less commonly [ɔː], [ɑː], [ɔ̃], in *blancmange*.
[68] EPD only [æ] in *chaffinch*.
[69] Already in Daines 1640 before *r*+cons.: see Dobson, §§42, 43.

final -r and -s Cooper gives a short vowel. A long vowel is certainly recorded in all positions, however, in the 18th century.

The pronunciation [aː] is nowadays used without exception before final -r and r-groups. In other positions [æ] also appears not infrequently beside [aː], and indeed [æ] gained ground in the course of the 19th century. In less common words like *aspect, asterisk, castigate, drastic, plastic* etc., many of which had [æː] in the 18th century, [æ] is now the prevailing pronunciation, while others like *mastiff, pastor, pasture* show variation.[70] However, some everyday words also have chiefly or exclusively [æ]; e.g. *ass, bass* (the fish, and 'bast'), *lass, mass* 'bulk' and the name of the church service.[71] Others, such as *class, glass, last* etc., which usually have [aː], are occasionally pronounced with [æ].[72] This variation is an old one. 18th century orthoepists (such as Perry 1776, Scott 1786, Walker 1791) frequently give [æ] in words of this kind. This [æ] may be to [aː] as PresE [ɔ] is to [ɔː] in words like *cross, lost* (cf. §75). [æ] may in part be explained as a reaction against the new pronunciation [aː]. Other variants, e.g. [à], exist beside [aː] and [æ].

On words like *quaff, waft,* see §27.

§47 In a few cases [aː] derives from ME *a* in other positions.

Not entirely clear is the [aː] in *answer, ant* (nowadays mostly pronounced [ænt], however),[73] *slant*. The influence of words like *chance, grant* is likely. *Answer*, judging by ME spellings like *aunswere* etc., and Hart's transcription *aunsuer*, seems to have had [au] beside [a] in ME and EModE.

On forms like *can't, shan't,* see §286.

Contraction no doubt explains [aː] in the shortened form *ma'am* from *madam*; [maːm] was still a common pronunciation in 'polite' circles at the beginning of the 19th century.

The origin of the [aː] in *father, rather,* is disputed. The long vowel, 18th century [æː], is usually explained as a result of contamination. Both words varied in EModE between a short and long *a* (ME *ă* and *ā*). Hart and Gil, e.g., have both quantities in *father*, Gil both in *rather*. It has been conjectured that, perhaps in the 17th century, [fæːðər] arose from a blend of [fæðər] and [fɛːðər]. This is doubtful,

---

[70] EPD also (less commonly) [ɑː] in *drastic, plastic*; only [ɑː] in *pastor* and *pasture*.
[71] EPD also (less commonly) [ɑːs] 'esp. as term of contempt'; only [æ] in *mass* 'quantity of matter', but also [ɑː] (less commonly) in *mass* the church service.
[72] Not in these words in EPD.
[73] EPD 'rarely' [ɑː] in *ant*.

however. Perhaps here also lengthening occurred;[74] cf. [ɔː] in *office*, *water*, etc., §75. [aː] in *lather* is late.

e-vowels and e-diphthongs

e in *bed*

§48 Late ME *e* represents:

1. OE (ON) *e*, *eo*: e.g. *bed*, *nest*, *Thames* (OE *Temes*, with *a* from Lat. *Tamesis*); *heaven*.
2. OE (ON) shortened *ē*, *ēo*, *ǣ*, *ēa*: e.g. *fed*, *fellow* (ON *félage*),[75] *breast*, *led*, *Edward*.
3. OE (East-Saxon) *e* < *y*: e.g. *bury* (OE *byrgan*), *left* (the direction), *merry*, *shed* (sb.).[76]
4. OF, Lat. *e*: e.g. *accept*, *pledge*, *dress*; *desert*, *level*, *nephew*.
5. OF *eo* (*eu*): *jeopardy*, *Leonard*, *leopard*.

In ModE [e] often appears instead of *a* through the influence of the spelling. In late ME [e] before [r] became [a]. The spelling *e* (*ea*) was often preserved, however (cf. also §25, 4), and this has often carried the pronunciation [e] with it. In earlier ModE numerous words were pronounced with [a, æ] which today have [e, ɔː]; e.g. *certain*, *Guernsey*, *herald* (EModE *harold* etc.), *servant*, *serve*, *verdict*. Sometimes *e* was written for an [a] which had not arisen from the English change of *e* > *a*, as in *Berkshire* (OE *Bearruc-*), still pronounced with [aː] today, and in *merchant*, *perfect* (EModE *merchant*, *marchant*, *perfit*, *parfit* < OF *marchant*, *parfait*). In words like *earth*, *search*, [ɔː] goes back to ME *ę̄* (§57).

§49 Late ME *e* has usually given [e]. Examples: *bed* [bed], *set* [set], *Thames* [temz].

The short *e* has probably remained substantially unchanged throughout the ModE period. Today it is mostly pronounced as a half-open [e], more exactly [è], i.e. almost like the German [e] in *Bett*. That the *e* was usually fairly close in EModE also is shown by the fact that *i* was sometimes written for it (as *e* for *i* in *bit*). Indicating a closer pronunciation of *e* than the Fr. or Du. *e* is the substitution of *a* [æ] for *e* in words like *rack* 'frame (etc.)' (Du. *rek*),[77]

---

[74] This is probably correct: see Dobson, §53. [aː] in *father* is found in the late 17th century, in *rather* not till the late 18th century.

[75] ODEE notes a late OE *fēolaga* < ON *félagi*.

[76] *Shed* (sb.) is of uncertain entymology: see ODEE.

[77] ODEE derives from Du. *rak*

reveille (often *revally* in the 18th and 19th centuries, and still sometimes pronounced [ri'væli];[78] < Fr. *réveillez*), *sack* (the wine) (Fr. *sec*).[79]

§50   Before final -*r* and *r*+cons. *e* has become [ə:]. Examples:
err [ə:(r)], *earl* [ə:l].

EModE [e] before [r] became a central vowel [ə] in the 17th
century. Such a vowel is attested by Wallis 1653 and by Cooper
1685, who gives the same vowel in *err* as in *hurt*. This change was
not, however, universal. In the 18th century many authorities still
teach the same *e* before *r* as in other positions, or a vowel different
from that in *turn*. We must assume two developments. In certain
circles [e] before *r* became [ə] and fell together with the vowel in
turn; this development subsequently prevailed. In other circles the
[e] remained first of all unchanged, to become in the 18th century a
central vowel which was not identical with the vowel in *turn* but
which was perhaps similar to the German *e* in *Gabe*. About 1800 [ə]
was lengthened to [ə:] at the same time as the [r] was lost (cf. §99).

In *bury*, *merry* etc., [e] remained unchanged; [ə:] in *erring* and the
like is due to the influence of *err* etc.

ę̄ in *leaf*

§51   Late ME *ę̄* represents:
1. OE *ēa*: e.g. *cheap, east, leap, stream.*
2. OE *ǣ* (<WG *ai*), ON *ǣ*: e.g. *heal, leave, wheat; seat* (ON *sǽte*).
3. OE *ǣ* (<WG *ā*): see below.
4. OE (ON) *e, eo*, in an open syllable: e.g. *beneath, eaves, even*
   (adj.), *speak, steal.*
5. ON *ei* before *k*: e.g. *bleak, steak, weak.*
6. OF *eé*: e.g. *dean, veal.*
7. OF *e* before *l*, before consonant groups and double consonants,
   and in originally unstressed syllables: e.g. *conceal; beast; pearl,
   search; preach; cease* (Fr. *cesser*), *beak* (Fr. *bec*); *Hebrew, lever.*
8. AN *e* from *ai, ei*: e.g. *ease* (cf. Fr. *aise*), *please, reason, treat;
   eagle, eager; increase* etc.
9. OF *ę̄u* before a labial and *ch*: e.g. EModE *Beamont* (<*Beau-
   mont*), *phlegm* (OF *fleume*), *Beauchamp*, nowadays [bi:tʃəm].
10. Lat. *e* in an open syllable: e.g. *complete, equal, glebe, scene.*

---

[78] EPD gives [æ] as the usual pronunciation. *a*-forms are found from the 17th
century.
[79] These examples do not prove that [e] was close, however; and there is
evidence the other way (see Dobson, §72).

In late (EModE) loanwords the reflex of ME ę̄ [eː] was substituted for every Fr. or Lat. *e*: e.g. in *obscene, scheme, sincere, supreme, theme*.

The products of ME ẹ̄ and ę̄ ([eː] and [iː]) were on the whole kept strictly apart in EModE. Indeed, a marked tendency is noticeable in the 16th century to distinguish the two by different spellings, ę̄ by *ea*, ẹ̄ by *ee, eo, ie*. However, this distinction was not consistently carried through: e.g. *e* was used for both sounds. The EModE spellings have mostly been kept quite accurately, so that PresE *ee* or *ie* usually indicates EModE ẹ̄ [iː], *ea* EModE ę̄ [eː].

§52 Variation between ẹ̄ and ę̄.

WG *ā* appears in OE as Saxon *ǣ*, Anglian-Kentish *ē*. OE *ǣ* gave ME ę̄, OE *ē* ME ẹ̄. Both developments are represented in the standard language. In EModE some words varied between ẹ̄ and ę̄: e.g. *leech, read, yea. Bleat, breathe, weapon*, e.g., seem usually to have had ę̄; *deed, eel, even(ing), greedy, needle, seed, sheep, sleep, street*, ẹ̄.

ME ẹ̄ before *r*, probably in late ME, frequently became ę̄. ę̄ is attested particularly often in EModE before *r*+cons., as in *earl, earth, fierce*. Orthoepists record it frequently also in *dear, hear, weary* (e.g.), and spellings like *appear, clear*, EModE *chear*, etc., indicate that it was common in others too. As for words with WG *ā*, *there, were, where* had apparently only ę̄,[80] while others, like *bier, fear, year*, varied.

More or less obscure is the variation in a few cases like *even* (adj.) (OE *efn*), *tear* (sb.) (OE *tēar*). *Near* (EModE ę̄, ẹ̄), however, goes back to OE *nēar* and *nēr*, *eke* 'also' (EModE ẹ̄ and ę̄) to OE *ēac* and (Angl.) *ēc*.

EModE *discreet, extreme*, with ẹ̄, are ME loanwords from OF; *discrete, extreme* with ę̄ are EModE loanwords.

§53 Late ME ẹ̄ mostly fell together *c.* 1700 with ME ī [iː], and has given PresE [iː]. Examples: *leaf* [liːf], *reason* [riːzn].

ME ę̄ was an open *e* [ɛː]. In the 16th century this had not yet become close *e*, since French authorities compare the sound with the open and not with the close Fr. *e*. On general grounds, however, it may be assumed that at least towards the end of the century ME ę̄ had been raised to about half-open *e* [èː]; about this time ME *ā* had been raised to [æː] or [ɛː]. About the middle of the 17th century

---

[80] Except for *where* in MS A of the *Welsh Hymn*, and in northern dialects. *Were* here, of course, is from the ME stressed form.

(Wallis 1653) close *e* [eː] is attested for certain.[81] Cooper 1685 pairs the sounds in *wean* and *win* as long and short. Since he still distinguishes the sound in *wean* from that in *feel*, the former was clearly extra-close, an [eː] similar to that in Danish *se*, or possibly [ɪː]. About 1700 the unambiguous falling together with ME *ę̄* [iː] is attested.[82]

§54 In four words—*break, great, steak, yea*—ME *ę̄* has become PresE [ei].

In these words ME *ę̄* fell together with the reflex of ME *ā*. The ancestor of the PresE pronunciation is first recorded with certainty after 1700 (Lediard 1725). The new pronunciation became fully established already in the 18th century. It is doubtful whether [ei] in all four words is to be explained in the same way. The archaic *yea* may have been remodelled on the sense-related *nay*. *Steak* derives from ON *steik*, and [ei] may have developed from ME *ai*. *Break, great*, are usually explained as dialectal forms. In many dialects the reflex of ME *ę̄* has completely fallen together with the reflex of ME *ā* (e.g. in Irish). According to others the change to [iː] was prevented by the preceding [r]. In support of this view it may be advanced that according to Cooper 1685 and others *scream* was often pronounced with the reflex of ME *ā* about 1700. Cf. also [ɔː] for [oː] §80.

§55 Usually ME *ę̄* before *r* also fell together with ME *ę̄* and has given PresE [i(ə)]. Examples: *ear* (organ of hearing), *rear* (vb), *shear* (vb), *spear, adhere, austere, cohere, serious, sincere, sphere*.

Strangely enough the falling together with ME *ę̄* under [iː] took place earlier before [r] than in other positions. Thus Butler 1633 has [iː] in *shear* (vb) and *spear*; he mentions [iː] in *ear* as incorrect pronunciation. Cooper has [iː] before *r* almost everywhere; e.g. in *ear, sear* (vb), *besmear, spear*.[83]

§56 In some cases ME *ę̄* before [r] has become PresE [ɛ(ə)], i.e. in *bear* (sb. and vb), *pear, swear, tear* (vb), *wear* (*ę̄* < OE *ĕ*), in *ere* (OE *ǣ* < *ai*), and in *there, were, where* (OE *ǣ* < WG *ā*).

The origin of the present pronunciation can be traced back to the 16th century. Bullokar 1580 ff. has the reflex of ME *ā* in *bear* (sb.) and *ear* 'to plough'. Chapman *c.* 1600 rhymes *swear, were*, with

---

[81] It is not certain that Wallis had [eː]: see Dobson, §§113–14 and n. 1.

[82] For a very different view of the history of ME *ę̄*, see Dobson, §§106 ff. For an explanation of the anomalous *break, great, steak* (see §54 below) on the basis of phonaesthetic theory, see M. L. Samuels, *Transactions of the Philological Society*, 1965, pp. 36–8.

[83] Dobson (§122) would explain such cases as due to earlier ME raising of *ę̄* to *ę̄* before *r*.

rare, care. Cooper 1685 gives the reflex of ME *ā* in *bear, pear, swear, tear, wear, ere, there, were,* and also *shear.* In the 18th century the new pronunciation is widely attested. It is not clear why the change to [iː] did not take place in these words. As far as *ere, there, where, were* are concerned, it may however be noted that they are often unemphatic, as a result of which shortening of the vowel often occurred. In *bear* etc. a lowering, perhaps from [ɛː] to [æː], seems to have taken place already in the 16th century.

Hair [hɛə], ME *hēr,* OE *hǣr,* has been influenced by the Fr. loanword *haire* 'hair shirt'.

§57 The pronunciation varied in EModE particularly before *r* + cons. In general, ME *ę̄* was shortened in the EModE period, and *er* became [ər], whence [əː]. Examples: *earl* [əːl], *search* [səːtʃ].

However, the long vowel is frequently attested in earlier ModE. The long vowel occasionally became [iː]. Here also [iː] is recorded remarkably early, e.g. by Hodges 1644 in *beard, pearl, perch.* Only in *beard* and *pierce* has [iː] survived; [biəd, piəs]. *Fierce, Pierce, tierce,* all with [iə], may also belong here (cf. §52), but this [iə] may also go directly back to ME *ę̄.* Sometimes the vowel fell together with the reflex of ME *ā.* This development is shown in Cooper 1685 in *beard, earl, search,* etc., by Lediard 1725 in *beard, earl, early,* and by Johnston 1764 still in *beard.* Perhaps the PresE [gɛəl] for *girl* is a survival of this development; the basic form would have been ME *gę̄rl* < OE *gerle.*[84]

ę̄ in *see*

§58 ME *ę̄* represents:
1. OE *ē*: e.g. (< WG *ę̄, e*) *he, me, here*; (< *ǣ*) *feed, queen, steed, sweet*; (< umlaut of *ēa*) *hear, need, steel*; (< *e* before *ld* etc.) *field, shield, yield*; (< *ēa* before *k*) *leek*; (< WG *ā*) *cheese* etc. (cf. §52).
2. OE *ēo,* ON *iū, iō*: e.g. *be, bee, creep, learn, see, meek* (ON *miūkr*).
3. ON *œ*: e.g. *seem.*
4. OE *ĭ, ў,* in an open syllable: e.g. *beetle, evil, week, weevil.*
5. OF *e*: e.g. (finally or before a vowel) *agree, degree,* names of

---

[84] The ME variants suggest earlier [y], and an OE **gyrela, *-e* has been proposed. But ModE [gɛəl] (now rare) certainly suggests derivation from ME *gę̄rl(e),* which is difficult to derive from the proposed OE forms. Ekwall's OE *gerle* is conjectural.

letters like *b*, *c*, *d*; (<Lat. *a* before *r*) *appear, cheer, peer* (sb.);
(<Lat. *e* in learned words) *Eve, Greek, metre, proceed*; (AN
e = Central Fr. *ie*) *brief, feeble, fierce, grief.*

6. OF *ue*: e.g. *beef, people, reprieve.*

In late loanwords the [iː] derived from ME *ę̄* often represents foreign *i*.
Examples: *esteem* (Fr. *estimer*), *seel* 'blind' (Fr. *ciller*),[85] *mien* (Fr. *mine*);[86]
caprice, fatigue, machine, police. Oblige often had [iː] in the 18th century;
PresE [ai] is a spelling-pronunciation.[87] In late loanwords Fr. *ie* also is
sometimes represented by [iː], as in *cannoneer, grenadier, pioneer.*

On the relationship between ME *ē̦* and *ę̄* in EModE, early change
to *ę̄* before *r*, and the writing of the sound, cf. §51 f.

§59   ME *ē̦* has usually become [iː], more exactly [ij]. Examples: *be*
[biː], *feed* [fiːd].

ME *ę̄* [eː] must have begun to move towards [iː] in the 15th century,
as rhymes (*ē:ī*) and spellings (*i* for *e*) show.[88] About 1500 [iː] or [ɪː] is
attested for certain. In the *Welsh Hymn* (*c.* 1500), and in Salesbury
1547 and Hart 1569 the sound is represented by *i*; Palsgrave 1530
and Bellot 1580 identify or compare it with Fr. *i*. A close quality is
certainly attested by Cooper 1685, since he distinguishes between the
quality of the vowels in *fill* and *feel*. Later, [iː] was diphthongized to
[ij]; this pronunciation, which is today the predominant one,[89] is
attested by Batchelor 1809.

§60   Before [r], or the [ə] deriving from it, [iː] was not diphthongized but somewhat lowered and shortened. In narrow transcription
the vowel is often represented by [ɪ], but usually the symbol [i] is
thought satisfactory. Thus *here* [hiə(r)], *fierce* [fiəs]. This development
has also taken place in words like *idea, theatre.*

The diphthong [iə] has a tendency to become [jəː]. Thus [djəː] is
heard for [diə] 'dear'. After [j], the [j] from [i] is lost: *year* is often
pronounced [jəː].

[85] ODEE: OF *ciller* or Med. Lat. *ciliare.*

[86] ODEE regards *mien* as probably from *demean* (sb.) with later assimilation
to Fr. *mine.*

[87] This is very doubtful: *oblige* is a 14th-century adoption, so [ai] is to be expected in this word.

[88] ME [eː] must have become [iː] by about 1450: note that the *Welsh Hymn*
is earlier than *c.* 1500. Ekwall's reference to *ē:ī* rhymes is mistaken, since ME *ę̄*
and ME *ī* remained distinct phonemes and could never have rhymed together
accurately.

[89] More accurately [ɪi] now.

ẹu in *dew*

§61 Late ME (EModE) *ẹu* represents:
1. OE *ēaw*: e.g. *dew, few, hew, shrew*.
2. OE *ǣw*: e.g. *lewd, mew* 'seagull'.
3. OE *eow*: e.g. *ewe, sew*.
4. OE *ef* in *newt*.
5. OF *eau*: e.g. *Beau-* in *Beaulieu, beauty, pewter*.
6. OF *ẹw* in *ewer, sewer* 'drain'.
7. Lat. *eu*: e.g. *Deuteronomy, eunuch, Europe, neuter*.

Deuce,[90] *feud* are of uncertain etymology.

In some words (e.g. *sew, shrew*) the pronunciation frequently varied still in earlier ModE between *ẹu* and *ọu*, or the products of these; *ẹu* represents OE *ēaw, eow* with a falling diphthong, *ọu* represents OE *eāw*,[91] *eow* with a rising one. Alongside *ewe* the variant *yowe* (< OE *eowu* with a rising diphthong) survived into the 18th century.

§62 Late ME *ẹu* fell together before 1700 with the reflex of ME *ēu*, and has become [juː, ju, uː, u]. Examples: *dew* [djuː], *ewer* [juə], *shrew* [ʃruː].

The first element of the diphthong in *dew* was, in the 16th century at least, often identical with the vowel in *leaf*; the diphthong is therefore to be analysed as [ɛːu] or [èːu]. This first element developed to close [eː][92] and then to [iː, i]. At the stage [iu] the diphthong fell together with the reflex of ME *ēu*. This falling together occurred earlier than the falling together of ME *ẹ̄* and ME *ẹ̄*, due perhaps to the fact that the first element of [iu] from ME *ẹu* was an open *i* [ɪ]. The complete falling together is already attested by Cooper 1685. For the later development see ME *ēu*.

ēu in *new*

§63 ME *ēu* represents:
1. OE *ēow* (*ıow*): e.g. *brew, clue, hue, knew, leeward,*[93] *true*.
2. OE *īw*: e.g. *steward, Tuesday, yew*.

[90] ODEE: OF *deus*.
[91] Ekwall *eaw*.
[92] This (intermediate) stage must have been a very brief one.
[93] EPD notes that the nautical pronunciation is ['lu(ː)əd, 'lju(ː)əd], otherwise ['liːwəd].

D

3. OE *ōh*, *ōg* in *drew*, *slew* etc. (cf. §250 f.).

The following fell together with ME *ēu*:

4. OF (AN) *eu*: e.g. *adieu*, *blue*, *due*, *fewel*,[94] *gules*, *Jew*,[95] *jewel*, *lieu*.
5. OF *iv*: *eschew*, *sue*.
6. OF *u* [y]: e.g. *duke*, *rude* etc.
7. OF *ui*: e.g. *bruit*, *fruit*, *June*, *pew*.
8. Lat. *u* in an open syllable: e.g. *curate*.

ME *ēu* was still distinguished from Fr. *u* in the 14th century. Chaucer avoids rhymes between the two. When he links OF *eu*, *iv* etc., and Fr. *u* in rhyme this is probably because they had fallen together in AN. No distinction was made in late ME between ME *ēu* and Fr. *u*. Probably ME *ēu* became [iu], more exactly perhaps [iːu] or [ɪu], in the 15th century, and this diphthong was substituted for Fr. *u*.[96]

§64 Late ME *ēu* [iu] has given PresE [juː, uː], more exactly [juw, uw]; before [r], however, [u], more exactly [ʊ]. Examples: *new* [njuː], *rude* [ruːd], *cure* [kjuə].

Several authorities attest for the 16th and 17th centuries an apparently falling diphthong [iu] or perhaps more exactly [ɪu]. Thus Hart 1569 has the transcription *iu*. Butler 1633 writes *kneew*, *sneew* etc., and gives *ee* the sound-value of a short *i*. Price 1668 has the transcription *iw*. Finally Cooper 1685 analyses the diphthong as *e* in *weal* or *i* in *will* plus *u*. A falling diphthong is still in use dialectally. A rising diphthong [iu] or [juː] is perhaps indicated by transcriptions like *you*, *kyou* (*kiou*) for *u*, *q* in Holliband 1566 (Ellis 838) and Mason 1622, and proved by *yoo* for the letter *u* in Hodges 1644. Miège 1685 mentions *yuse* beside *use* as less correct pronunciation. The pronunciation [juː] is also indicated by the [ʃ] recorded from the 16th century in *sure* etc. (cf. §156).

In the 18th century [juː] was fully established. Presumably this [juː] derived partly from a new shift of [iu] to [juː]. PresE [sjuːt] = *suit*, e.g., presupposes 17th century [siut]; PresE [ʃuə] 'sure', on the other

---

[94] Presumably for PresE *fuel*.

[95] In fact < OF *giu*.

[96] Luick (§§399.2 and 407.3) has shown that the change of ME *ēu* to [iu] is to be dated *c*. 1300. The substitution of the English diphthong [iu] for OF [y] is a separate issue. Most scholars now believe that it normally occurred in ME itself in East Midland dialects; but in cultivated speech (such as Chaucer's) it may not have been accepted till the 15th century.

hand, presupposes 16th century [sjuːr].[97] On the later history of the [uː], cf. §84 ff.

The older observations on the pronunciation of ME *ēu* frequently disagree. A few French authorities maintain that *u* (*ew*) etc. are spoken as *iu*, which taken literally would mean [iy]. Many scholars also assume such a pronunciation. Probably, however, *iu* is an inaccurate transcription. It is notable that some authorities (e.g. Mason 1622, Festeau 1672) use *iu* as well as *iou* (*you*) in transcriptions.

The reflex of ME *ēu* (and Fr. *u*) is often compared with Fr. *u* [y]; e.g. by Smith 1568, Bullokar 1580, Wallis 1653. Some scholars hold that in the 16th and 17th centuries the pronunciation [yː] existed alongside [iu] etc. Especial weight has been given to Wallis's evidence; according to him English and Fr. *u* are simple sounds, *iu* in Spanish *ciudad* is a compound one. Against this observation, however, has been set that of Wilkins 1668, according to whom Fr. *u* is only used in French, and is very difficult for foreigners (e.g. Englishmen) who do not know the sound. This contradiction is all the more striking because Wallis and Wilkins lived at the same time in the same Oxford College.[98] Probably Wallis did not perceive the difference between [iu] and Fr. [y]. Earlier observations which seem to point to [yː] are also suspect.[99]

§65   After the change to [iuː, juː] the [i] or [j] was often lost. In the PresE standard language this is regularly the case after [j, ʃ, tʃ, dʒ, r] and after a consonant+[l]; e.g. in *chew, Jew, rue, blue* [dʒuː, tʃuː] etc. The loss is attested with certainty by Lediard 1725.[1] He mentions the loss after [d, t, l, n, s], e.g. in *dew, steward, lewd, new, suit*. Eighteenth century pronouncing dictionaries also (e.g. Scott 1786) sometimes mention [uː] in words like *duke, suit* etc. Today [uː] in words like *duke, suit* etc., is very common in popular London speech, in northern English, and in American.[2] In the standard language the usual pronunciation is [juː]; but after [l, s], [uː] is in

---

[97] But there is no need to assume a new phase of [iu]>[juː]; see Dobson, esp. §§185, 187–8.

[98] Ekwall seems to be mistaken here. Wallis and Wilkins were indeed in Oxford at the same time, Wallis as Savilian Professor of Geometry from 1649, Wilkins as Warden of Wadham College 1648–59. But Wallis had been educated at Emmanuel College, Cambridge, and was incorporated an Oxford M.A. from Exeter College; Wilkins had been educated at New Inn Hall and at Magdalen Hall, Oxford.

[99] But see Dobson, esp. §§182–4, 187–9.

[1] There is earlier evidence than Lediard, in 'homophone' lists; see Dobson, §185 (p. 707).

[2] But also common after *s* in RP (see EPD and note 3 below).

use in most words alongside [juː]; e.g. *allude, Lucy, lunatic, revolution, absolute, superior, Susan.*[3]

i-sounds

i in *sit*

§66 Late ME represents:

1. OE (ON) *i*: e.g. *bit, live, sit, window.*
2. OE (ON) *y*: e.g. *fill, first, kitchen, sister.*
3. OE shortened *ī, ȳ*: e.g. *fifteen, wisdom; hid.*
4. OF (Lat.) *i*: e.g. *prince, simple, pity, riches,*[4] *village.*
5. Early ME *e*, especially before *ng, nk*: e.g. *England, English, linger*[5] (cf. OE *lengan*), *fringe* (OF *frenge*),[6] *ink* (cf. Fr. *encre*);[7] in *hint* (OE *hentan*), *rid* (OE *hreddan*),[8] perhaps in *pretty*; after palatals in *chill* (OE *c(i)ele*),[9] EModE *yes, yesterday, yet* (often still with *i* in the 18th century).
6. OE *ē* by later shortening, as in *riddle, silly*: cf. also §16.

§67 Late ME *i* has usually given [i], more exactly [ɪ]. Examples: *bid* [bid], *linger* [liŋgə].

The short *i*, as rhymes and spellings indicate, had probably an open quality [ɪ] already in Late ME,[10] at least in certain positions. In the 16th century [ɪ] is attested in certain positions by the Welshman Salesbury 1547, but in other positions [i].[11] An open quality for *i* in all positions is proved for the second half of the 17th century by the fact that Cooper 1685 gives the short *i* in *will* etc. as identical in quality with the long vowel in *weal* (cf. §53). For the later periods of ModE only an open quality is to be assumed for short *i*.

§68 Before final [r] and [r]+cons. [i] became [ə], whence PresE [əː]. Examples: *stir* [stəː(r)], *girl*[12] [gəːl], *bird* [bəːd].

---

[3] EPD has only [uː] in *Lucy*, and predominantly [uː] in *allude, lunatic, revolution, absolute*, and *Susan* ('rarely' [juː] here, and only [uː] in *Susanne*); predominantly [juː] only in *superior.*

[4] Ekwall: *richess.*

[5] Frequentative of *leng* (vb) < ON *lengja.*

[6] But also OF *fringe.*

[7] OF *enque.*

[8] *rid* is in fact from the rare OE (*h*)*ryddan* (not ON *ryðja* (*pace* ODEE) which is cognate with it) and thus belongs in Ekwall's category 2.

[9] The sb. *chill* comes from the vb *chill* (of obscure origin), and is not the reflex of OE *c(i)ele.*

[10] *i* must have been open [ɪ] in ME and throughout the ModE period.

[11] Salesbury's use of [i] in certain positions is dialectal, and largely a reflection of Welsh pronunciation: See Dobson, I, pp. 14–15.

[12] Though there were other forms: see earlier, §57 and note 84.

Already in the 16th century *u* is not infrequently found instead of *i* before *r*, especially where *i* goes back to OE *y*, as in *first*, *stir*, *thirst*, or where *ir* has arisen from *ri*, as in *bird*, *dirt* (OE, ME *bridd*, *drit*). Here, as the evidence of grammarians and rhymes (*stir : cur* etc.) show, the pronunciation was [u].[13] These cases are to be distinguished from the later change of [i] > [ə].

From the 17th century onwards we find two developments of *i* before *r*. On the one hand *ir* fell together with *er* but remained distinct from *ur*; on the other, [i] before [r] became a central vowel, and *ir* fell together with *ur*, perhaps in [ər]. The latter development is attested by most of the English authorities (e.g. Hodges 1644, Price 1668, Cooper 1685). In the 18th century the statements of the authorities frequently differ. According to some (e.g. Nares 1784) *ir* and *er* had fallen together with *ur*, perhaps in [ər]. This development later became general. According to others (e.g. Elphinston 1765), *ir* had fallen together with *ur*, perhaps in [ər], while *er* was pronounced differently. According to yet others (e.g. Walker 1791) *ir* in certain words had fallen together with *ur*, in others with *er*. Walker records an *e* 'which approaches to the sound of short *u*' in *birth*, *chirp*, *firm*, *gird*, *girl*, *virgin*, *virtue* and others, as against '*u*' in *birch*, *bird*, *first*, *sir*, *stir* and others. Similar statements are made by other orthoepists. This strange division has been explained in the following way: that '*u*' [ə] comes from EModE *u* [u] (see above), while '*e*' (on the pronunciation cf. §50) in the 17th century derives from [i].[14]

Simultaneously with the loss of [r], [ə] was lengthened to [əː]; cf. also §99.

In words like *miracle*, *stirrup*, [i] is used today. In earlier ModE [e] or [ə] is occasionally attested in these words. Walker 1791 and Smart 1836 still have [ə] in, e.g., *syrup*, [e] in, e.g., *panegyric*, *squirrel*. Also [i] after [r] sometimes became [ə] in *threepence*, pronounced, according to Elphinston 1765, either *thruppence* or *thrippence*.[15]

ī in *die*

§69   ME *ī* [iː] represents:

---

[13] Note that this [u] was a common variant to [ɪ], not the invariable pronunciation.

[14] Ekwall's discussion here does not take sufficient account of the origins of the 18th century observers: e.g. Elphinston was a Scot.

[15] There is no evidence of [ə] in *threepence*. Ekwall appears not to have known the pronunciations [θrupəns, θrʌpəns] which attest EModE *ŭ* [ʊ] by rounding of *i*.

1. OE (ON) *ī*: e.g. *Christ, life, ride*; (< *ĭ* before *ld, mb* etc.) *child, climb, blind.*

2. OE (ON) *ȳ*: e.g. *hire, hive*; (< * y̆*) *kind, mind*; *mire* (ON *mȳrr*), *sky*.

3. OE *ig, yg*: e.g. *nine, scythe, tile*; *lie* 'untruth' (<OE *lyge*),[16] *rye*.

4. OE *ē(a)*, *ē(o)*+*g*, *h*: e.g. *eye, high* (OE *ēage, hēah*), *fly* (OE *flēogan*), *thigh* (OE *þēoh*), *island* (OE *ēgland*); ON *ē* (*ǣ*)+*g, j*, e.g. *die, sly* (ON *dœja*,[17] *slœgr*).

5. OF, Lat. *i*: e.g. *cry, lion, desire, nice, sign, vine, bible, pint; climate, viscount.*

6. EME *ę̄*, especially before *r*: e.g. *briar* (OE *brēr*), *choir* (OF *cuer*), *entire* (OF *enter*), *friar* (OF *frere*), *die* (sb.) (OF *de*), *contrive* (OF *contruev-*).

7. EME *ĭ* before [çt]: e.g. *bright, fight, right.*

§70   ME *ī* has given PresE [ai]. Examples: *die* [dai], *right* [rait], *fire* [faiə].

The diphthongization of ME *ī* must have begun in the 15th century and was complete *c.* 1500. The *Welsh Hymn c.* 1500,[18] Salesbury 1547, Hart 1569, Bellot 1580 use the transcription *ei* (*wein, reid* = *wine, ride*), which suggests a diphthong [ei] or (less probably) [əi]. The statements of a few authorities (Palsgrave 1530, Smith 1568) seem on the other hand to indicate a monophthong [iː]; it is very doubtful, however, whether these are to be taken literally. The stage [əi] is attested with certainty from the middle of the 17th century, e.g. by Wallis 1653 and Cooper 1685; in these and various later authorities the first element of the diphthong is compared with the vowel in *cut* or the unstressed vowel in *better*. Foreigners in the 17th and 18th centuries often compare the diphthong with German or Fr. *ai*. Perhaps the pronunciation varied as late as this, as it still does today. Today the first element is mostly analysed as a mid, central vowel [ə] (Jespersen, Western, and others).[19] But a low

[16] The noun *lie* is in fact a 13th century derivative from the verb (OE *lēogan*), replacing OE *lȳge*; see ODEE.

[17] Perhaps the best discussion of this disputed etymology is in D'Ardenne, *An Edition of . . . Seinte Iuliene*, pp. 146–7, who assumes assimilation of ON *deyja* to native models such as OE *wrēgan*. See also ODEE.

[18] Before 1500; see note 2 to §4(c) above.

[19] [əi] is almost exclusively regional now, but Gimson *Introduction*, §7.23 notes that even nowadays a more centralized and retracted variety of the first element may still be heard from those using a more conservative type of RP.

vowel is often used; phoneticians describe such pronunciations as
[ài, ai, æi].

§71   A separate development has taken place in *ay* 'yes', EModE
I, today sometimes pronounced [aːi]. This pronunciation, or its
ancestor, is recorded from the 18th century onwards.[20]

o-sounds and *o*-diphthongs

o in *god*

§72   Late ME *o* represents:
1. OE (ON) *o*: e.g. *dog, off, loft.*
2. OE *ō* from early shortening: e.g. *fodder, rod,*[21] *soft.*
3. OE *ā* by ME shortening: e.g. *long, song, holiday.*
4. OF, Lat. *o*: e.g. *coffer, lodge; bottle, forest, jolly, poverty.*

§73   ME *o* has usually given PresE [ɔ]. Examples: *dog* [dɔg], *long*
[lɔŋ], *poverty* [pɔvəti].

ME *o* is usually assumed to have had the sound-value of a mid
back vowel [ò]. PresE [ɔ] is a low back vowel with slight rounding.
This pronunciation existed already in the 16th century, as is shown by
Bellot's comparison of the English *o* with Fr. *a* (cf. his transcriptions
Tames, chart for *Thomas, short*). Since Hodges 1644 *o* in *god* has been
compared in quality by numerous authorities (Wallis 1653, Cooper
1685, etc.) with the [ɔː] in *law*, which clearly proves [ɔ]. Later foreign
observers also identify or compare the English short *o* with Fr. (or
German or Du.) *a*. German *a* in loanwords like *baxen, Frack* (from
English *box, frock*), and English [ɔ] in *dollar* (recorded from the 16th
century from Du. or LG *daler*), *yacht* [jɔt] from Du. *jacht*[22] are
explained by the similarity between [ɔ] and [a].

Some scholars explain the comparisons of English *o* in *god* with Fr.
(German, Du.) *a* by the assumption that in the earlier standard language
an [a] due to unrounding was also in use alongside [ɔ] or [o]. It is a fact
that [a] appears instead of [ɔ] in many dialects and in American English,
and an unrounded vowel, probably [a], was common as a fashionable
pronunciation in the 17th and 18th centuries; cf. spellings like *bax, nat,
stap*, for example, for *box, not, stop* in Sheridan's comedies. We have,
however, no reason to suppose that this [a] was general in the standard
language.

[20] Only [ai] now according to EPD.
[21] This should be under 1. Late OE *rodd* is not developed, as Ekwall appears
to have assumed, from earlier *rōd*; see ODEE.
[22] ODEE: EModDu. *jaght(e)*.

§74 In a few isolated cases ME *o* has become PresE [æ]; e.g. in *nap*, *sprat*, *strap* (ME *noppe*, *sprot*, *strop*). These forms have probably been borrowed from dialects in which ME *o* had become [a]; [æ] has then been substituted for [a]. *Egad* (from *A God*) probably derives from the fashionable pronunciation mentioned above.

§75 ME *o*, EModE [ɔ], has frequently been lengthened to [ɔː]. Examples: *corn* [kɔːn], *off* [ɔːf], *frost* [frɔːst].[23]

The lengthening occurred particularly before final [f, r, s, θ] and before [f, r, s]+cons.: so, e.g., in *off*, *cough* (cf. §163), *for*, *loss*, *cross*, *broth*, *froth*, *often*, *soft*, *corn*, *order*, *frost*, *lost* etc. The [ɔ] from [a] after [w] also took part in the lengthening; e.g. in *war*, *warm*, *dwarf*, *swath* etc.

The lengthening is attested by Daines 1640 in *warn*, *warp* and the like, by Cooper 1685 in *off*, *corn*, *frost* etc. At first [ɔ] remained alongside [ɔː] before [r]. When [r] was lost, [ɔː] became regular in words like *for*, *horn* etc.; in others the variation still persists. However, only [ɔ] is in use, or at least [ɔː] is very rare, in certain words, particularly in disyllables or polysyllables like *gospel*, *hospital*, *impostor*, *ostrich*, *prospect*, but also in other cases, like *doff*, *Goth*. In some of these [ɔː] is recorded in the 18th century. Words like *posset*, *possible*, are only recorded with [ɔ]. On the other hand [ɔː] is recorded in *coffee*, *offer*, *office(r)* etc., in the 18th century, and is still occasionally to be heard in such cases.[24]

Gone, *shone*, are sometimes pronounced [gɔːn, ʃɔːn].[25] This lengthening is probably late.

[ɔː] in *water*, attested by Cooper 1685, is obscure. It is usually explained as due to contamination. The length of the *a* in this word varied in EModE; Bullokar 1580 ff. and Gil 1621 give both long and short. [wɔːtə] may have arisen in the 17th century from [wɔtər]< [watər], and [wɛːtər]. However, [ɔː] instead of [ɔ] from [a] occurs also elsewhere, e.g. in *squadron* according to Elphinston 1790 and Walker 1791; in *quadrant*, *quadrate* according to Walker. Perhaps in all cases lengthening is of [ɔ] to [ɔː].

Wrath, today [raːθ, rɔːθ],[26] has its [ɔː] probably from the influence of the adj. *wroth*, EModE [wrɔθ].[27]

---

[23] But [ɔ] is very common in *off*, *frost* etc. nowadays.

[24] Rarely, and appears to be going out of use.

[25] EPD gives [gɔːn] as a subsidiary pronunciation; only [ɔ] in *shone*.

[26] [rɑːθ] appears to be obsolete now except in Scotland and in the name *Cape Wrath*. EPD gives [rɔθ] as the usual pronunciation, [rɔːθ] as subsidiary.

[27] On [rɔːθ] and other abnormal lengthenings, see Dobson, §53.

ǭ in *no*

§76 Late ME *ǭ* represents:

1. OE (ON) *ā*: e.g. *boar, boat, ghost, comb*.
2. OE (ON) *o* in an open syllable: e.g. *bore* (vb), *before, hope*.
3. OF (Lat.) *o*: e.g. *close, note*; *noble*; *coach, poach*; *sport* (cf. further §79); *poem, poet, ocean*.

In the 16th century the spelling *oa* began to be used to mark the reflex of ME *ǭ* as distinct from [uː] from ME *ǭ*, while *oo* was used only for [uː] or [u]. The distinction was not consistently carried through, however. Thus *o* remained in frequent use, and as much for *ǭ* as for *ǭ*.

§77 Late ME *ǭ* has a rule given [ou][28] except before *r*. Examples: *boat* [bout], *coach* [koutʃ].

The value to be assigned to the ME long vowel in *no*, usually indicated by *ǭ*, is in general probably that of an open *o*-sound similar to the PresE [ɔː] in *law*. In the 16th century, however, the vowel must have begun to move towards close *o* [oː]; we may assume the quality of a half-open *o* [ò:]. Already *c.* 1600 the long open [ɔː] had in fact developed from [au], and the reflex of ME *ǭ* remained carefully distinguished from it. Close *o* [oː] is recorded about 1650 (Wallis 1653, Cooper 1685). The PresE diphthong [ou], more exactly [oːu], has developed from this. It is first mentioned by Batchelor 1809.

§78 Before [r], or the [ə] arising from it, ME *ǭ* has given PresE [ɔː(ə)]. Examples: *boar* [bɔː(ə)], *glory* [glɔː(ə)ri].

ME *ǭ* before [r] developed for a long time along with *ǭ* in other positions. A more open quality before [r] was first noticed by phoneticians in the 19th century; PresE [ɔː] here has thus developed very late. Probably the lowering began more or less simultaneously with the diphthongization of the [oː] in *no* etc.[29] The change to [ɔː] has occasionally taken place before an [ə] which has not developed from [r]; e.g. in *boa* [bouə, bɔːə].

Eighteenth century [oː] which had developed from EModE [uː] or EModE [oːu] also took part in the development to [ɔː]; e.g. *course* [kɔː(ə)s], *floor* [flɔː(ə)], *four* [fɔː(ə)].

§79 Thus different vowels, [ɔː] and [oː], were still used *c.* 1800 in *law*

[28] In PresE usually [əu]: see Gimson, *op. cit.* §7.25.

[29] The quality of this vowel before *r* is likely to have been more open throughout the modern period, but was allophonic until the *r* was lost and so escaped notice till then.

and *boar*; [ɔː] was also used in *horn* etc. (cf. §75). The distribution of the sounds [ɔː] and [oː] *c.* 1800 in the standard language (and still in northern English and Scottish) was as follows:

[ɔː] represents chiefly:

1. EModE [au]: e.g. *law, slaughter.*
2. EModE lengthened [ɔ]: e.g. *corn, for, horse, morning, short, thorn; absorb, orb(it), cord, order, torch, gorge, organ, corner, scorn, fortune, sort,* and others.

[oː] represents chiefly:

1. ME *ǭ*: e.g. *before, glory, store*; in French words like *divorce, force, remorse, porch, forge, pork, fort, port* (with derivatives like *support*), *sport.*
2. ME *ǭu* in *four.*
3. ME *ǭ*, EModE [uː]: e.g. *door* etc.
4. ME *ū*, EModE [uː]: e.g. *course, court.*

Some words varied, especially participles such as *born, torn* etc. (cf. §234). *Form* had [oː] in the sense 'bench' (< ME *fourme*), [ɔː] in the sense 'shape'. Otherwise the above distinction between [oː] and [ɔː] was preserved with only unimportant exceptions by the orthoepists of the 18th century (like Nares 1784 and Walker 1791). Many dictionaries retained it long after; in the OED it is indicated by different symbols.

§80 In *broad, abroad* the change to [oː, ou] has not taken place;[30] the PresE pronunciation is [brɔːd]. In this case ME *ǭ* has fallen together with the reflex of ME *au*. The earliest orthoepical evidence for this irregular pronunciation is given by Hodges 1644.[31] Still earlier evidence is Spenser's rhyme *abroad : fraud. Groat* (the coin) was also generally pronounced with [ɔː] till about 1800. [ei], earlier [eː], instead of [iː] in *break, great* (§54) is to be compared with this [ɔː] instead of [ou]. [ɔː] can be explained as a dialectal pronunciation, or as due to the influence of the preceding [r].[32]

§81 In earlier ModE there are some traces of the falling together of ME *ǭ* with ME *ǭ* under [uː]. Cooper 1685, e.g., has [uː] in *boar, born.*

This [uː] has not survived. However, it is possible that PresE [ʌ] in *none, nothing, struck* has derived from shortening of this [uː].[33] This explanation is probably the right one for *struck*; cf. §215. In *none, nothing*, only [oː] or [ɔ] is attested in the 16th and 17th centuries; Bysshe 1702 is the first to give the pronunciation [ʌ]. However, this [ʌ] can be explained differently. E.g. it may be the product of

[30] This is not quite correct. (*A*)*broad, groat* are found with regular [oː] in EModE alongside [ɔː] (and [ɔ] too in the case of *groat.*)

[31] It may be recorded in one instance by Gil 1619; but see Dobson, §53.

[32] Dobson (§53) explains as lengthening of shortened ME *ǭ.*

[33] This is the explanation adopted by Dobson, §§36, 150–1.

shortening of [oː]; an *o*-type of pronunciation for the vowel in *cut* is often attested in the 17th and 18th centuries (§97). The American forms *hull, hum*, instead of *whole, home*, in which shortening of [oː] is apparently to be assumed, would be comparable. The curious pronunciation [rʌlək][34] for *rowlock* may belong here; *rullock* is recorded in the OED from 1821.

§82 The development of ME *ǭ* in *one, once* [wʌn, wʌns] is strange. In the 16th and 17th centuries orthoepists for the most part attest [oː] or [ɔ] for both. Cooper 1685 still gives [oːn] as the only form.[35] PresE *alone, atone, only* with [ou], *nonce* [nɔns] still show the regular development. A form with initial *w-* is attested by Hart 1570 for *only* (oddly enough), which he writes *uonli*. Otherwise this initial *w-* is first mentioned by observers in the second half of the 17th century. That it was common earlier, however, is shown by the fact that already in the 16th century *such a one* was frequently written as well as *such an one*. The spelling *wone* for *one* already occurs in the 15th century.

The form with initial *w-* has mostly the vowel [ʌ], less often [ɔ] and [æ]. Hart's *uonli* probably means [wɔnli].

The initial *w-* is evidently to be connected with the common dialectal diphthongization of ME *ǭ* to [oə, uə] etc., whence also [wə, wa] etc. Analogous are the dialectal forms *wuts, hwutter* for *oats, hotter* mentioned by Cooper 1685. The diphthongization is found especially in western dialects, but also in districts close to London. Signs are not entirely lacking that it had also been in the process of entering the standard language, but only in *one, once* has it been successful. The analogous diphthongization of ME *ẹ̄* (> [iə] etc., whence [jə] etc.) which is occasionally attested by earlier observers (in *yerth, yerb* for *earth, herb*), has left no traces in the contemporary language.[36]

ǭ in *do*

§83 ME *ǭ* represents:
1. OE (ON) *ō*: e.g. *do, doom, moor, spoon; boon, root*; (< *ŏ* before *ld, rd*, etc.) *gold* (cf. §17); *board, ford, forth, afford, sword*.
2. OE *ā* after *w* in *two, who* (*whom, whose*), *womb*.

---

[34] EPD gives [ɔ] as normal in *rowlock*, [ʌ] as subsidiary.
[35] But also *wun* as 'barbarous speaking' 1687.
[36] This is not quite true; [jəː] exists as a rare pronunciation of *ear*. On these [w] and [j] glides, and the pronunciations [wʌn] etc., see also Dobson, §§428–31.

3. ON *ǫu*: e.g. in *loose*.

4. OF *o* in a few early borrowings, such as *boot* (type of shoe), *fool*, *Moor*, *rook* (in chess), EModE *Rome* [37] (still with [uː] in Walker 1791), *throne*.[38]

5. OF *ov* in *poor* (<*povre*).

6. OF *ou*, *u* in *move*, *proof*, *prove*[39] (cf. Fr. *mouvoir*, *prouver*).

7. EME *ŭ* occasionally in an open syllable, as in *door* (OE *duru*), EModE *above*, *love* etc.

8. EME *ū* as in *droop*, *room* etc.: cf. §103.

In late loanwords the reflex of ME *ǭ*, EModE [uː] was substituted for Fr. *ou* [u] or nasalized *o*; examples: *accoutre*, *Louvre*, *tour*; *poltroon*, *pontoon*.

§84 ME *ǭ* has usually become [uː], more accurately [uw], except before [r]. Examples: *do* [duː], *prove* [pruːv].

ME *ǭ* must already in the 15th century have begun to move towards [uː]. The stage [uː] was reached for certain *c.* 1500.[40] The *Welsh Hymn* (*c.* 1500) and Salesbury use the transcription *w*, the Welsh symbol for [uː]. Hart 1569 writes *u*. Bellot 1580 equates the vowel in *do* with Fr. *ou* [u]. This [uː] remained unchanged till *c.* 1800; about this time (in Batchelor 1809) the pronunciation [uw] is recorded, and this is still current.

§85 Before [r], or the [ə] derived from it, ME *ǭ* has usually become PresE [ɔː], less commonly [u] (more accurately [ʊ]). Examples: *floor* [flɔː(ə)], *forth* [fɔː(ə)θ], *moor* [muə], *poor* [puə].[41]

ME *ǭ* became [uː] before [r] in late ME and fell together with ME *ū* before *r*+cons. (as in *course*; cf. §103). In the 16th century [uː] seems to have been the usual pronunciation; occasional spellings, however, such as *board* for *boord*, *coarse* for *course*, indicate that [uː] had already begun to revert to [ɔː]. [ɔː] in *door* may go back, at least in part, to OE *dor*. In the first half of the 17th century our authorities still attest [uː], and give [ɔː] in isolated words only; Gil 1621 has [ɔː], e.g., in *board*, *poor*, *door*. In the second half of the century some authorities, like Wallis 1653 and Cooper 1685, give

[37] Also OE *Rōm*.

[38] Also EModE [ɔː].

[39] *proof* owes its vowel to *prove*. The phonology of *move*, *prove* is disputed. They seem to have ME *ǭ*, which, however, cannot be explained from OF. See Dobson, §36 n. 3.

[40] This stage had probably been reached by *c.* 1450: cf. ME *ę̄* above. The *Welsh Hymn* is earlier than 1500; see note 2 to §4(c).

[41] Also [mɔə, mɔː], [pɔə, pɔː]; see EPD, and §86 below.

[uː], others, like Miège 1685, [oː]. In the 18th century [oː] became general and this has become [ɔː] (cf. §78).

§86 In a few words, however, [uː] remained. This is the case with *boor, moor, poor,* which mostly have [uː] in the 18th century. The retention of [uː] has been attributed to the preceding labial, but this is rather doubtful. In some less common words written with *ou,* like *amour, gourd, tournament,* [uː] is due to the influence of the spelling. *Tour* is a late loanword. In *your* the common [uː] is due to the influence of *you.* In addition, the [uː] resulting from the change of [iu] to [juː] remained unchanged in words like *cure, jury, pure, secure, sure.* EModE *shore* for *sewer*† 'public drain' seems really to be a different word (= *shore* 'beach') (OED).[42]

In these and similar words [uː], probably in the 19th century, has been somewhat lowered and shortened to [u], more accurately [ʊ]. A tendency for this [ʊ] to become lowered to [o] and even [ɔː] is distinctly noticeable in contemporary speech, particularly among the younger generation. Thus today [mɔː(ə), pɔː(ə), ʃɔː(ə)] etc., are frequently heard beside [muə, puə, ʃuə].

§87 [ou] instead of [uː] is a spelling pronunciation in words like *behove* (OE *behōfian*), *mote* 'must' (OE *mōt*), names like *Coke* (= *Cook*), *Pembroke* (usually [-bruk]), *Walpole* (really *-pool*). Unexplained is *woke* [wouk] from OE *wōc* (§249).[43] On *don't* [dount] see §286.

ǭu in *know*

§88 Late ME ǭu represents:

1. OE *āw*: e.g. *blow* ('to puff' etc.), *crow, mow* (vb), *slow.*
2. OE (ON) *āg*: e.g. *owe, low* (ON *lāgr*).
3. OE *ōw*: e.g. *blow* 'to bloom', *glow, grow.*
4. OE (ON) *og*: e.g. *bow* (sb.), *flown.*
5. OE *ēaw, ēow, eow* (> *eāw* etc.): e.g. *four, trow, show, sow, sew* 'to stitch', cf. §61.
6. OE (ON) *ā, o* before [x]: e.g. *dough, brought, cough, thought, trough.*
7. OF *ou* in a few problem cases like *mould* (for metal) (Fr.

---

† Ekwall notes: '*Shoreditch* has nothing to do with *sewer,* as has been generally supposed. Forms like *Shoredich* are recorded from the EME period.'

[42] It is clearly a different word; see ODEE.

[43] OED suggests analogical influence of *broke, spoke.*

moule),[44] *scroll* (ME *scrowe*, OF *escroue*), *solder* (cf. Fr. *souder*), *soldier* (ME *soudiour* etc.).[45]

8. EME *o*, *ǭ* before final *l*[46] and *l*+cons.: e.g. *bowl* 'dish', *folk*, *bold*, *sold*.

The change to *ǭu* failed in pet-names like *Doll*, *Moll*, *Noll* (*Dorothy*, *Mary*, *Oliver*), and the same applies to *doll* (child's toy) and *poll* 'parrot'. Influence of the full names (*Dorothy* etc.) or by-forms like *Dolly*, *Molly* is to be assumed. *Loll* [lɔl] from ME *lollen* is obscure. Late loanwords, or those influenced by the original Latin form, like *extol*, *solve*, *devolve*[47] etc., show mostly [ɔ]. *Revolt*, however, is pronounced [ri'voult].

9. EME *u* before *ld*, *lt*: e.g. *shoulder*, *boult* (Fr. *buleter*), *poulterer*, *poultry* (cf. ME *pulte*, Fr. *poulet*).

§89   ME *ǭu* fell together in the 17th century with ME *ǭ*, and has usually given PresE [ou], before *r* [ɔ:]. Examples: *blow* [blou], *folk* [fouk], *sold* [sould]; *four* [fɔ:(ə)], *towards* [tɔ:(ə)dz].[48]

Most observers in the 16th century keep the reflexes of ME *ǭu* and ME *ǭ* apart, and describe a diphthongal pronunciation for ME *ǭu*. The correctness of these observations is corroborated by the fact that comparatively rarely was *ow* written for *o*, or *o* for *ow*; spellings like *roe* 'spawn' for *rowe*, *throe* for ME *throwe* are comparatively late. The diphthong was composed of the long *o* in *no* and a [u], and must therefore have been very similar to the PresE [ou] in *no*. Beside this diphthongal pronunciation there seems also to have been a monophthongal one in the 16th century; this was identical with the *o* in *no*. A diphthongal pronunciation is attested still in the 17th century. Thus Gil 1621 preserves the distinction between ME *ǭu* and *ǭ*, and Wallis 1653 and Cooper 1685 declare both [o:u] and [o:] to be permissible pronunciations of ME *ǭu*. On the other hand Hodges 1644 gives only the monophthongal pronun-

[44] ODEE takes this as presumably a metathetic alteration of OF *modle* (whence ModF *moule*).

[45] As OF *ou* was [u], and gives ME *ŭ* or *ū*, late ME *ǭu* in these words is comparable to its occurrence in category 9 below. But the inclusion of *solder* here is dubious; though OED gives a pronunciation [souldə], EPD has only [sɔldə] and (less commonly) [sɔ:də, sɔdə], and these latter are all historical pronunciations, explicable by ME and OF variants of the word.

[46] Ekwall's 'final *l*' is a mistake and should read 'before double *l*'; *bowl* is from OE *bolla*. Diphthongization did not take place before a single *l*, e.g. in *bole*, *coal* etc.

[47] EPD gives [-təul] as commoner than [-tɔl] in *extol*; only [ɔ] in *solve*, *devolve* (though [ou], [əu] can also be heard).

[48] Also commonly [tu'wɔ:dz], a re-formed pronunciation.

ciation. Towards the end of the 17th century ME *ǫu* had normally fallen together with ME *ǫ* and has shared its subsequent development.

According to Jespersen (*M.E.G.*, 11. 4) PresE [ou] goes directly back to EModE [oːu]. The falling together with the reflex of ME *ǫ* would in this case have occurred through the diphthongization of *ǫ* in EModE.

§90   ME *ǫu* before [xt] has become PresE [ɔː]. Examples: *daughter* (OE *dohtor*), *brought, sought, thought, wrought* etc. [dɔːtə, brɔːt] etc. The pronunciation [ɔː] in *brought* etc. is generally attested from Hodges 1644 onwards. Earlier observers (such as Hart 1570, Gil 1621, etc.) denote the same vowel or diphthong as in *know*, and this pronunciation is occasionally attested later. *Daughter* has usually been spelled with *au* since about 1500, and all the orthoepists of the 16th and 17th centuries record [au] in this word or developments of [au] such as [ɔː] and [æf] (cf. §163). In this word ME *ǫu* fell together early with ME *au*. Now, rhymes like *thought : taught* occur in EModE as well as in late ME. Probably ME *ǫu* in *brought, thought* etc., also became *au* in late ME, though the spelling *ou* was retained; from this particular [au], which only occurred before [xt], [ɔː] resulted. The [oː(u)] attested in EModE represents a parallel development.

On words like *cough, trough*, see §163.

§91   [au] instead of [ou] in *prow* (of a ship) is due to the influence of the spelling[49] (cf. Coleridge's rhyme *prow : blow*; [ou] still in Smart 1836); so also *prowl*[50] (ME *prollen*, [oː] Nares 1784). Vice-versa, [ou] instead of [au] in *bowl* 'ball' (Fr. *boule*) can be explained as a spelling-pronunciation; blending with *bowl* 'drinking vessel' (OE *bolla*) is also possible.

oi (ui) in *joy, boil*[51]

§92   Late ME, EModE *oi(ui)* represents:
1. OF *oi(ui)*: e.g. *choice, join, joy* (cf. below).
2. OF *ǫ* before *l* mouillé: e.g. *spoil*.
3. OF *u* [y] in a few cases like *recoil* (cf. Fr. *reculer*), *roister* (Fr. *rustre*),[52] EModE *moile* beside *mule* (the animal).

[49] See ODEE for a different suggestion.
[50] For a different explanation, see Dobson, §169 n. 1.
[51] See also on this whole matter (which is very complex) Dobson, §§252–63.
[52] ODEE derives *recoil* from OF *reculer*, *roister* from OF *rustre*. Dobson explains the *oi* in these words as due to analogy.

4. Fr. *ou* etc. in *foil* 'to frustrate' (Fr. *fouler*),[53] *soil* (cf. OF *saoul* 'full')[54] etc.

5. Fr. *i* in *joist* (OF *giste*).

6. Du. *oei*, *ui*: e.g. *buoy* (Du. *boei*),[55] *doit* (Du. *duit*),[56] *hoy* (Du. *hoei*), *toy* (Du. *tuig*);[57] *i* in *hoise*.[58]

7. OE *ȳ* in *boil* 'swelling', *groin* (part of the body) (OE **grȳnde*[59]). The origin of *boy* is obscure (perhaps native).[60]

§93 Late ME *oi(ui)* has become PresE [oi]. Examples: *boy* [boi], *spoil* [spoil].

In earlier ModE there were two types of pronunciation of ME *oi* (*ui*). PresE [oi] derives from EModE [oi]. This diphthong has probably changed very little during the ModE period. The first element is usually about [ò] today. Beside [oi] there were several diphthongs in earlier ModE whose first element was an [uː] or [u] or some sound developed from them. In the 16th century [uːi] occurs in Bullokar 1585; the existence of [ui] is not so certain. In the 17th century Gil 1621 has [uːi], Cooper 1685 [ui]. From [ui], at the same time as the unrounding of the [u] in *cut* (cf. §97), there developed what was probably [ʌi], attested by Wallis 1653, and thence [əi], recorded, e.g., by Cooper 1685. At this stage the reflexes of ME *i* and EModE [uːi, ui] fell together. A still earlier falling together might be indicated by Spenser's rhymes such as *boil* : *mile*; but these are hardly altogether pure rhymes.[61] More important is the fact that spellings like *boil* for *bile* 'swelling', *groin*, *hoist*, *joist*, for *grine*, *hise*, *giste* appear early (according to the OED *boil* in 1529, *groin* 1587, *hoist* 1509,[62] *ioist* 1494).

---

[53] ODEE regards this word as perhaps from AN **fuler*, variant of OF *fouler*.

[54] Ekwall's gloss *sättigen*, i.e. 'sate', 'fill' shows that he meant the word recorded in OED as *soil* v.[3], which in fact means 'to feed animals on fresh-cut fodder' (originally for purgation), formerly also 'to fatten up fowls'; but his suggested etymology is very doubtful. The origin of the word is unknown.

[55] ODEE: probably from MDu *bo(e)ye*, *boeie* (Du *boei*).

[56] ODEE derives *doit* (a small Dutch coin) from MLG *doyt*.

[57] *toy* is of unknown origin: it is unlikely to be from Dutch in view of the English sense-development (see OED). It may be from French; see Dobson, §256 n. 3 and the references given there.

[58] ODEE: probably from Du. *hijschen* or LG *hissen*, *hiesen*.

[59] ODEE: perhaps a transferred use of OE *grynde* 'abyss'.

[60] See Dobson, §256 n. 3 and the references given there.

[61] These are in fact probably good rhymes, based on a separate development of ME *ui* > *wī*, mentioned by Ekwall below (§95).

[62] In fact *hoise*.

In *boil*, *groin*, *oi* has perhaps developed from ME [yː];[63] *groin* may also have been influenced by *loin*. On the other hand, *oi* in *hoist*, *joist* clearly indicates early falling together of ME *oi* with ME *ī*, probably in lower class speech; *hoist* is a nautical word, *joist* a technical term of carpentry.

The pronunciations [oi] on the one hand and [uːi] on the other were not used indiscriminately; on the contrary, in some words (e.g. *choice*, *joy*) only [oi] was used, in others (such as *poison*, *spoil*) [uːi] etc. was common. As late as the second half of the 18th century even educated speakers frequently used [əi] in *boil*, *spoil* etc., and poets unhesitatingly rhymed *toil* with *pile* etc. (and even *joy*: *I* etc. by analogy). In the last decade of the 18th century, however, under the influence of the spelling and as a result of the efforts of teachers of pronunciation [əi] was displaced by [oi]. In popular London speech, on the other hand, [əi] or [ai] is still often used.[64]

§94 The relationship between the two pronunciation types is complicated. The following statements take into consideration only etymologically unambiguous words of French origin.

The following words have only, or almost exclusively, [oi]; [oi] represents:

1. OF *ǫi < au + i̯*: *choice*, *cloister*, *joy*, (*rejoice* etc.), *noise*.
2. OF *ǫi < ei*: *coy*, *employ*, *exploit*, *poise*, *loyal*, *royal*, and others.
3. AN *ǫi < Lat. ǫ + i̯* (=Central Fr. *ui*): *annoy*, *oyster*, *void*.
4. OF *ǫi < Lat. ō, ŭ + i̯*; in unstressed syllables also *ǫ + i̯*: *boisterous*, *coif*, *moist*, *voice*.

[uːi, ui, əi] or the like are attested by, e.g., Bullokar 1585, Gil 1621, Hodges 1644, Cooper 1685 and others in the following words whose sources are:

1. OF *ǫi* before *n*: e.g. *coin*, *join*, *loin*, *ointment* (Fr. *ǫi* was nasalized and has diverged in development from oral *ǫi*; cf. Fr. *coin* and *voix*).
2. OF *ǫ* before *l* mouillé: e.g. *boil*, *soil*, *spoil*, *toil* (Fr. *bouillir* etc.).
3. OF *ǫi* in an unstressed syllable in *poison*.
4. OF *ǫi* before *l*: e.g. *oil*, *soil* 'earth'; but these often have [oi].

The distinction is thus an etymological one, and must depend on the situation in ME and AN. EModE [oi] derives apparently from

---

[63] It is difficult to see how. It is more likely that all these words developed pronunciations with [ui] and [oi], and spellings with *oi*, by analogy; so Dobson, §259.

[64] No longer, apparently.

ME *oi*, [uːi] from ME *ui*. Numerous spellings testify to ME *ui*, such
as *despuilen, bruyle, puison* etc.

Now, with one group of words with [oi] existing alongside another
group with [uːi, ui] it is not surprising to find the one sometimes
influencing the other. However, influence on the [oi] group is seldom
demonstrable. On the other hand words of the second group are
often attested with [oi]; thus Gil 1621 has [oi] and [uːi] in *join, toil*,
and others. Clearly, spelling-influence can also be assumed.[65] The
treatment of AN *o̦i* before *l* (in *oil, soil*) is not clear; perhaps [oi] is
the regular development and [uːi] is due to the influence of *boil*,
spoil etc.

As for the other words, it may be mentioned that *boy* never, as
far as is known, had [uːi],[66] but on the other hand *buoy* often did.

§95   *Special developments.*

The spelling *buoy* denotes a pronunciation [bwoi] that still exists,[67]
and is mentioned by Cooper 1685, for example. [w] has developed
after the [b]; Wallis 1653 mentions cases like *pwot* for *pot*, etc.

[wiː] sometimes developed from [uːi, ui] in ME. Hart 1569 transcribes *buoy, hoy* as *buei, huei*, and Hodges' transcription of the
reflex of ME *ui* is perhaps to be interpreted as [wəi]. EModE spellings
like *quine*, and Lediard's [kwəin] for *coin* are to be compared. [wi]
also occurs for ME [ui], as in *quince* (the fruit), which is really
from *coin*.[68]

u-sounds

u in *bull, cut*

§96   Late ME *u* represents:
1. OE (ON) *u*: e.g. *buck, come, full*; (< *eo, io, y* after *w*) *cud*,
   wood, work, world.
2. OE (ON) *ū* with early shortening: e.g. *dove, duck* (vb), *shove*,
   sung; *Thursday*.[69]

---

[65] A ME [oi] variant should be assumed also: see Dobson, §252.

[66] But some dialectal developments appear to depend on it: see Dobson,
§256 n. 4.

[67] Not, apparently, any longer, though it is given as a variant in OED.

[68] By *coin* Ekwall does not mean the surviving English word of that form, but
the obsolete *coyn* (OF *cooin, coin*, modern Fr. *coing*), from the plural of which
quince developed.

[69] The inclusion of *Thursday* here, separated from the other words, implies that
it is from ON and has original *ū* (cf. ON *þórsdagr*); in fact it is from OE *þu(n)res-
dæg* and has original *ŭ* (cf. OED and Campbell, *OE Grammar*, §474), and thus
belongs in category 1.

3. OE *y* (*i*) in the neighbourhood of labials: e.g. *church, clutch, cudgel, furze, shut, woman.*

4. OE *o* (*a*) before *ng*: *among, -monger*. On *ŭ* < ME *ō̦*, cf. §16.

5. OF *u, o, ou* [u]: e.g. *number, plunge; couple; disturb, adjourn, butcher, colour, comfort, country.*

6. Occasionally OF *u* [y]: e.g. *humble, judge, just; duchess, punish, study.*

7. OF *ui* (*oi*) before *sh*: e.g. *bushel* (OF *boissiel*),[70] *cushion, usher.*

§97 ME *u* became for the most part unrounded and has given [ʌ]. Examples: *cut* [kʌt], *mud* [mʌd], *colour* [kʌlə]. Rarely it has remained unchanged as [u]. Examples: *full* [ful], *woman* [wumən].

The short *u* was probably already pronounced as an open *u* [ʊ] in late ME. Most 16th-century observers did not make a distinction between the vowels in *cut* and *full*, nor yet did Gil 1621 or Butler 1633. The beginning of the differentiation, however, certainly comes in the 16th century; Bellot 1580 compares the vowel in *up* with Fr. *o*, but that in *buck, book* with Fr. *ou* [u]. Hodges 1644 is the first Englishman to show this distinction.[71]

The statements about the pronunciation of the vowel in *cut* in the 17th and 18th centuries are conflicting. Frenchmen and Germans frequently compare the vowel with Fr. or German *o*. An *o*-sound similar to the impure Fr. *o* in *comme* is often used today by Americans and northerners instead of standard English [ʌ]. Such a sound may very well have been current in the earlier standard language. It is easy to imagine this sound deriving from [u] by weakening of the rounding and lowering to middle tongue-position. English observers of the 17th century (e.g. Wilkins 1668, Cooper 1685) frequently identify the vowel in *cut* with the unstressed vowel in *better*. This observation is hardly entirely accurate; Miège 1685, like Batchelor 1809, makes a distinction between these sounds, and they are still distinct today.

When the PresE unrounded vowel with the distinct *a*-quality developed is not clear. The fact that the Portuguese de Castro 1750 compares the vowel in *cut* with the Portuguese *a* has been taken as evidence for the existence of [ʌ] *c.* 1750. Spellings like *bungalow, pundit*, with *u* for the impure Indian *a*-sound, which are found from the second half of the 17th century, also perhaps indicate [ʌ].[72]

---

[70] Also *buissiel.*

[71] But there is some evidence of a distinction in Daines 1640.

[72] *punkaw* 'punkah' occurs as early as 1625; cf. Dobson, §59 n. 6, and §93 n. 3.

These do not amount to certain proof, however, since the impure *a*-sounds can also be mistaken for an impure *o*-sound.

§98 The unrounding often failed after labial consonants, especially before [l, ʃ]. ME *u* remained here as [u], more accurately [ʊ]. Examples: *bull, bullet, pull, pulpit, Fulham, wolf, wool; bush, bushel, push, pudding, put, woman, wood;* cf. also *cuckoo, cushion.* [ʌ] occurs between labials and *l* particularly in less familiar words, as in *bulb, bulk, pulp, pulse.* In earlier ModE variation between [u] and [ʌ] is sometimes recorded. Cf. also §16.

§99 Before final [r] and *r*-groups ME *u* became [ə], whence PresE [əː] through loss of the [r]. Examples: *fur* [fəː(r)], *hurt* [həːt].

The vowel in *fur, hurt* was for a long time identified with the vowel in *cut,* and was no doubt very similar to it. The falling together with the vowel from [i] before [r] indicates, however, a shift of the *u* before [r] to a central vowel [ə]. With the loss of the [r] the [ə] was lengthened and evidently somewhat lowered. The [əː] in *fur* is rather lower than [ə] in unstressed syllables.[73]

§100 Not infrequently, when written *o*, historical [u, ʌ] have been replaced by [ɔ] or [ou]. Thus [ɔ] has been adopted in *accomplish, con* (OE *cunnan*), *grovel,* in the names *Bolingbroke* (earlier often *Bullingbrooke*), *Cromwell* (instead of *Crum-*)[74] and others. Variation between [ɔ] and [ʌ] still occurs in *bomb, bombast, combat, constable, frontier, sovereign.*[75] [ou] is used today in *coney* 'rabbit' (EModE *cunny* etc.), *wont* 'accustomed' (OE *gewunod*); *yeoman* (from *young man*; cf. OED).

In the prefixes *con-, com-,* as in *comparable, conscience,* [ɔ] is due chiefly to Lat. influence; we find the regular development of Fr. nasalized *o(u)* in *company, conjure,* with [ʌ]. The variation between [ɔ] and [ʌ] in words like *coral* (nowadays [ɔ], but [ʌ] in Cooper 1685), *polish* (nowadays [ɔ], EModE *pullish* etc.) originates in French, where *o* and *ou* in a pretonic syllable often interchange with each other.

ū in *now*

§101 ME *ū* represents:

1. OE (ON) *ū*: e.g. *cow* (sb.), *house, mouth;* (< *ŭ*) *pound* (sb.), *sound* (adj.), *mourn.*
2. OE *ug, ūg*: e.g. *fowl, youth; bow* (vb.).

---

[73] It is doubtful if this is so today, except where [ə] is in the vicinity of velar consonants.

[74] Though [ʌ] is still heard in *accomplish, grovel,* and *Cromwell,* and [u] though 'old-fashioned' in the first syllable of *Bolingbroke* (see EPD).

[75] Not nowadays in *bomb, bombast,* or *sovereign* (EPD).

3. OE *ōg, ōh*: e.g. *bough, plough*.

4. OF *u, ou* [u]: e.g. *vow, gout, hour*; *tomb*; *round, count*; *gourd, course, court*; *crouch*;[76] *coward, boundary*.

§102 ME *ū* has usually given PresE [au]; e.g. *cow* [kau], *mount* [maunt].

The diphthongization of ME *ū* (usually written *ou, ow*) must have begun in the 15th century and been complete by *c*. 1500. In the *Welsh Hymn* (*c*. 1500) and in Salesbury 1547 the spelling *ow* is used. Hart has the transcription *ou* (before *r* in *flour* etc. *oũ*), Bellot 1580 *au, aou*. In the 16th century the first element seems to have been usually an *o*-vowel.[77] This was later unrounded, and from Wallis 1653 onwards it is mostly identified with the vowel in *cut* or the unstressed one in *better*. A diphthong [əu] is still often used[78] alongside [au, àu]. In phonetic notation [au] is mostly used.

On [ʌ] in *enough* etc. cf. §163.

§103 The diphthongization often failed, and ME *ū* fell together— already in late ME—with ME *ǭ*, EModE [uː]. ME *ū* remained as EModE [uː]:

(a) Before *r* + cons.: e.g. *mourn, court, source*.
(b) Before a labial: e.g. *droop* (ME *droupen*), *stoop* (vb), *room, tomb*.
(c) Before [k]: e.g. in *brook* (vb), and with early shortening *duck*,[79] *puck, suck*.
(d) After [w] in *wound* (sb.) (OE *wund*), *swoon* (cf. OE *swōgan*),[80] *woo* (OE *wōgian*), all with [uː]; *wound* [waund] from *wind* has been influenced by *bound* : *bind*.
(e) In *you, your* (cf. Pronouns); in *youth* (ME *youthe*), often pronounced in EModE with the diphthong in *new* [iu]; hence regular [juːθ].
(f) In *uncouth* (with [uː] in Cooper 1685; obscure).

B. Vowels in Weakly-stressed Syllables

§104 Vowels in weakly stressed syllables show in all periods a strong tendency to be reduced, and in fact to become in ModE [ə] or [i]. Often this weakening is not fully carried through. Sometimes, instead of [ə, i], a sound between the original vowel and [ə, i] is used;

---

[76] Possibly; etymology uncertain, but likely to be French.

[77] For a different view, see Dobson, §160.

[78] Not now in RP.

[79] The ME variants in *duck* point to original variation in the quantity of the vowel (see ODEE).

[80] The words do not seem to be related; the etymology of *swoon* remains uncertain.

e.g. instead of [ou] a weakened [o] tending towards [ə], instead of [u] a fronted [u] with weak rounding, instead of [e] often a vowel between [i] and [e]. In general the [i] in unstressed syllables is rather lower than the [i] in *bit*. Definite rules as to the use of fully and partly weakened vowels cannot be laid down. In rapid speech [i, ə] are more common than in slower, more careful speech. The reduction occurs more readily in everyday words than in less common ones.

In syllables with secondary stress the original vowel often remains unaltered. Examples: *sublet, umbrella, undo* [ʌ], *recover* 'cover again' [iː], *autocrat, contract* [æ], *contrast, paragraph* [æ, aː], *placard* [aː], *essay* (sb.) ['esei], *alcohol, diphthong, dialogue* etc. [ɔ], *concord, escort, record* [ɔː], *paramour* [uə], *income, 'insult* [ʌ], *empire* [aiə]. In some of these the secondary stress may be due to the influence of related words (e.g. *'insult* ['insʌlt] after *in'sult* (vb)). This is clearly the case with, e.g., the [æ] in the second syllable of *adaptation*, [aː] in *departmental* (after *a'dapt, de'partment*), [ai] in *civilization* [sivilai'zeiʃən] etc. (after *civilize*).

I. WEAKENING

(a) In initial syllables

§105   Here weakening seems to have occurred fairly late, since the original vowels are often retained more or less unchanged.

a in an open syllable is mostly pronounced [ə], as in *about, ad'dress, lament*; in a closed syllable often as [æ] as well as [ə], as in *absolve, accent* (vb), *admire, anxiety*;[81] *ar* > [a, aː] as in *barbaric, cartoon, partake*, more rarely [ə][82] in very common words like *particular*.

o in open syllables > [o, ou] or [ə]: e.g. *hotel, notorious, obey, omit, professor*;[83] in closed syllables *o* > [ɔ] or [ə], as in *observe, obtain, October*.[84] In words like *obey* long *o* [oː] is often attested in the 18th century (e.g. in Sheridan 1780, Walker 1791), and short *o* [ɔ] in *observe* etc. [ɔː] is often shortened to [ɔ], as in *Australia, causality, portentous*.[85] The shortening is attested from *c.* 1700.

u > [ə], as in *subjoin*,[86] *suppose*; [uː] > [u] in *bouquet* [bu'kei],

---

[81] Not in RP now in *absolve, admire*.
[82] 1965 edn misprints [ɔ].
[83] Not now [ou] ([əu]) in *professor*.
[84] Not now [ɔ] in *observe, obtain*, but it is used in some words (e.g. *obscene*).
[85] Not now [ɔ] in *causality*, nor in *portentous* (or any other *-or-* words).
[86] Only [ʌ] today in *subjoin*; but *subject* (vb), e.g., varies.

routine[87] etc., EModE [iu] > [ju, u], as in *humane, museum, unite*
with [ju], *lucidity, superior* with [ju, u].

e mostly > [i], as in *effect, elate, betake, decide, engage,* but > [ə]
before [r]+cons., as in *fer'ment, per'ceive*. In EModE *e* was often
long in open syllables: [eː] in *decide, retain* etc., [iː] in *behold, betake*
etc. The EModE interchange between *en-, em-* and *in-, im-* (*embrace,
engage, im-, in-*) is due to the competition between Fr. *en-* (*em-*)
and Lat. *in-* (*im-*).

i mostly > [i]: e.g. *iniquity, irresolute; i* > [ə] before [r]+cons., as
in *cir'cumference*. In words of Latin origin *i* is frequently pronounced
[ai], as in *biography, gigantic, idea, librarian, tribunal*; the school
pronunciation of Latin has [ai] here.[88] In contemporary speech [ai]
is gaining ground in syllables preceding the stress; it is heard in
words like *digest, direct, finance, italics*[89] etc.

ai > [ə]; e.g. in *maintain,*[90] *saint* as in *Saint Paul's*. Earlier, *saint*
was sometimes pronounced [sint]; cf. *St John* [sindʒən], *St Clair*
[siŋklɛə], in which the first syllable has become stressed. Similarly
[i] in *mister, mistress* (< *maister, -es*) is derived from [ai] in proclitic
position.

(b) In medial syllables

§106   Here at an early date we find spellings indicating marked
reduction.

Front vowels and *ai, oi* have mostly become [i], as in *Alexander,
ancestor, cognizance* (Fr. *connaissance*),[91] *connoisseur,*[92] *parliament*
(ME *parlement*); however, before [r] the development was to [ə], as
in *Chesterton, every*, and in *levelling, marvellous, seventy* etc., after
level etc. However, [ə] is also heard, even in place of [i] in words
like *possible, unity*.[93]

---

[87] But also [uː].

[88] By the 'school pronunciation' Ekwall, writing in 1914, meant the traditional,
centuries-old, English pronunciation of Latin, then still dominant in English
schools, which explains the pronunciation of English words adopted from Latin.
But already a 'reformed' pronunciation was being introduced, and it is this which
is now used in almost all schools and universities. In the old traditional pronunciation [ai], as Ekwall says, was used in such Latin words as *biographia, gigantem*.

[89] Not now [ai] in *italics*.

[90] Often [ei] here now, probably under the influence of the spelling.

[91] In fact from OF *conis(s)aunce, conus(s)aunce*, variants of *conois(s)ance*.

[92] More usually with [ə].

[93] EPD gives only [i] here, though [ə] is to be heard.

a > [ə], as in *paradise, separate*; > [i] often in *character*. The change of [a] to [e, i] in *messenger* (cf. *message*) etc. had already taken place in ME.

o > [o] or [ə]; [o] is used particularly in less common words: e.g. *abolition, avocation, eloquence*;[94] [ə] is predominant in everyday words, as in *chocolate*,[95] *opposite, somebody*.

u [iu] > [ju, u], as in *argument, regular, prejudice*; > [ə] before [r], as in *conjurer, injury*. In EModE [iu] sometimes became [i], as in *manuscript*.[96]

(c) In final syllables

§107 All vowels before [r] tend to become [ə]. [r] is later lost after [ə]. Thus [ə] is heard in, e.g., *orchard, water, Berkshire, author, venture*.

Weakening before [r] is attested early; by orthoepists already in the 17th century (Hodges 1644, Cooper 1685, etc.); by spellings (e.g. *feauor* for *fever, lyar* beside *lier*, etc.) already in the 16th century. However, the stage [ə] was not reached in all terminations even in the 16th and 17th centuries. [ər] is recorded for *-our, -or* (in *endeavour, actor* etc.) right into the 17th century. The ending *-ure* in *creature, nature*, indeed often became [ər] in EModE; but at the same time [iur] or [juːr] remained, perhaps as a more 'refined' pronunciation, and later (perhaps in the 18th century) became PresE [jə], or combined with [s, z, t, d] to become [ʃə, ʒə, tʃə, dʒə]. Forms like [sensər, ventər] for *censure, venture* occur, e.g., in Cooper 1685 and are still found in the 18th century.

§108 The vowels *a* [a], *o, u,* usually become [ə] before other consonants also.

a > [ə], e.g. in endings like *-al, -an* (*final, ocean* etc.), in *breakfast, England, trespass* etc.; [ə] is recorded with certainty from the 18th century. Beside [əl, ən] syllabic [l, n] also occur, e.g. in *metal, pleasant*. The ending *-al* was often pronounced [aul, ɔːl] in EModE[97] (according to Hart 1569, Hodges 1644; cf. rhymes like *fall : general* in Shakespeare and others).

o > [ə], e.g. in endings like *-ock, -on, -ot* (*bullock, nation, bigot* etc.),

---

[94] Not now. EPD gives [ə] and [əu] in these words, with a variant [u] in the case of *abolition*.

[95] Frequently also [tʃɔklit], with syncope of [ə]. Syncope is also heard in *somebody*.

[96] Cf. also §112.

[97] The [a] thus undergoing the same development as in stressed syllables.

in *gallop, Europe, wainscot* etc. Instead of [ən], [n] often occurs, as in *bacon, button*. After palatal consonants [in] was not uncommon in earlier ModE instead of [ən], as in *cushion, pigeon, widgeon*[98] (Hodges 1644, Walker 1791, and others).

u > [ə], e.g. in endings like *-ous, -us*, e.g. in *famous, bolus*. Words like *beautiful, handful*, vary between [ful, fəl, fl].

§109 Final back vowels have been better preserved.

a > [ə] in words like *Anna, Candida, drama*; but [a] also occurs.[99]

ow in *follow, yellow* etc., varied in earlier ModE between [oːu, oː, o] and [uː, u], later [ə]. Bullokar 1580, Hodges 1644, Cooper 1685, and others, give one of the former pronunciations, Salesbury 1547, Lediard 1725, and others, one of the latter. We must suppose two types as current since the ME period. Today the usual pronunciation in educated colloquial speech is [ou, o]. This applies also to words like *Apollo, tobacco*.

ough (< *uh*) in *borough, thorough*, is usually [ə].

EModE [iu] in *issue, nephew* etc., [eːu] in *sinew* > [juː] > PresE [ju, u].[1]

§110 Front vowels before consonants have mostly become [i].

i > [i], e.g. *childish*; ME *ē̞*, EModE [iː] > [i], e.g. in *handkerchief, mischief*; ME *ī* > [i], e.g. *housewife* [hʌz(w)if], *sevennight* [senit].[2] There is much variation between [i] and [ai] in words in *-ice, -ile, -ine, -ite*.[3] We have [i] in *benefice, surplice, destine, discipline, infinite* etc., [ai] in *columbine, Valentine, finite, parasite* etc. Adjectives in *-ile, -ine*, like *fertile, hostile, finite*[4] vary a lot, but [ai] seems to be gaining ground.[5] [ai] is to be ascribed to Latin influence.[6] 18th century observers often have [i] where [ai] has now prevailed. [i] is often syncopated before [l, n], as in *pupil, cousin, raisin* [pjuːpl, kʌzn, reizn].

e > [i], e.g. in endings like *-ed, -es, -ess, -est, -et, -less, -let, -ness* (*naked, roses, heiress, fairest, poet, useless, violet* etc.). [i] is recorded

---

[98] And is still to be heard; EPD regards [i] as commoner than [ə] in *pigeon*.
[99] Rarely nowadays: not given by EPD.
[1] Also [juː].
[2] [hʌzif] now only in the sense 'needle-case'; otherwise [hauswaif]. *Sevennight* s no longer in use (cf. §138).
[3] Not now in the case of *-ice*, where very few words have [ai].
[4] Obviously *finite* is misplaced here. Ekwall gives no example of an *-ine* word, and presumably intended one like *pristine*, which was formerly pronounced with [in] (see OED in 1909) but now has only [ain].
[5] This trend has continued.
[6] Presumably not latterly, when influence of the spelling seems more likely.

with certainty from the 18th century onwards. [ə] also occurs in these endings and is predominant in *hundred, kindred*,[7] e.g., and often in *-less, -let, -ness*, and others. Before [l, n], *e* has mostly become [ə] or disappeared, as in *barrel, bushel, evil, barren, element* etc. However, [i] is found, especially before [n]; a few words, like *chicken, kitchen, linen, women* have only [i].[8] Walker 1791 records [i] very widely before [l, n].

ę̄ [eː] > [i] in *counterfeit, forfeit, surfeit* etc. These words had a long vowel in the final syllable in EModE which developed like [eː] in stressed syllables and may have been shortened early to [i]. [i] is attested from the 17th century on. The ending *-es* as in *Hercules, series*, EModE [eːz], has become [iːz] with occasional shortening to [iz].

§111 ME *ā*, EModE [æː, ɛː], belonged in EModE to the front vowels. This vowel occurs in endings like *-ace, -age, -ate* (*palace, cottage, private* etc.), but alongside short *a*. We find early weakening in *ducat, palate*, for example, EModE *ducket, pallet* (Hart 1569 *palet*). Otherwise weakening is first recorded in *-age*. Orthoepists testify to [idʒ] in the 17th century. Spellings like *cabbidge* appear in the 16th century, and in *porridge* (<*pottage*) this spelling has prevailed. The early appearance of the [i] is due to the palatal [dʒ]. The PresE pronunciation is [idʒ], as in *cabbage, image*. In the remaining endings the weakening is attested later. In the 18th century [e] or [ə] is given. The pronunciation still varies today between [i] and [ə]; thus *palace, private*, are pronounced [-is, -it, -əs, -ət]. Perhaps [i] goes back to EModE [æː, ɛː], and [ə] to EModE [a]. The long vowel has been retained in verbs in *-ate*, like *aggravate*, otherwise rarely, e.g. in *irate, ornate*.

§112 Diphthongs containing front vowels often become [i].

ai > [i] in *always*,[9] *captain, mountain, sovereign* etc.; here [i] is recorded with certainty in the 17th century. *Calais* already appears in EModE as *Calles, Callis*.[10] Alongside [in], [n] or [ən] occur, as in *captain, villain*.[11] Syncope of *ai* before [l, n] had often taken place already in ME, as in *battle, victuals, leaven, mitten* (< Fr. *bataille,*

[7] EPD gives only [kindrid].
[8] *kitchen* has also [(ə)n] now.
[9] Also [ei, ə] now.
[10] EPD gives [kælis] as 'old-fashioned', and [kælei] as more common than [kæli].
[11] [ə] in *captain* is not acknowledged by EPD; *villain* only [ə], but with [i] as a variant in its historical sense.

vitailles, levain, mitaine); cf. *boatswain, cockswain* [bousn, kɔksn].
Britain is [britn].

[iu] > [i] in *biscuit, conduit, lettuce, minute* (sb.), etc.; [i] is recorded
in EModE (in the 16th century and later). In some less common
words, like *latitude, tribute, verjuice*, [juː, uː] is heard. *Fortune* is
[fɔːtjun, fɔːtʃən].[12] Exceptional is *periwig*, EModE *perwig, -wicke,
-uke*, from Fr. *perruque*.

oi > [i] in *porpoise, tortoise*; [i] is given in these words by, e.g.,
Walker 1791. PresE pronunciation: [ə].

§113 Final *-e, -ey, -y* and the like > [i].

In *coffee, epitome, Galilee, Pharisee* etc., with EModE [eː], [eː, e]
were still pronounced in the 17th century, whence [i] or [iː]. The ME
terminations *-ę̄* (in *pitē* etc.), *-īe* (in *maladie* etc.) and *-ī* (in *honī*, OE
hunig etc.) probably fell together in late ME under *-ī*. In the 16th
century the pronunciation varied between [i, ei, iː][13] and in rhymes
these endings were coupled with words like *die* and *see*. Later, [i]
prevailed. The ME endings *-aie, -eie*, as in *abbey, valley* (ME *abbeie,
valeie*) were often pronounced in EModE with the diphthong or
vowel in *day*. In the 17th century [i] was certainly used here as well.
[i] also occurs in *Sunday* etc.

2. Loss of Vowels

§114 Loss of an initial vowel, or of an initial syllable also containing a consonant often occurs in ME. Typical cases are ModE
twit, down, dread (OE *ǣtwītan, of dūne, ondrǣdan*), *vantage, fend, gin*
(cf. *advantage, defend, engine*). In the ModE period such loss has
occurred rarely; late cases are *cute, rack, ticket, tinsel* (< *acute,
arrack*, Fr. *étiquette, étincelle*).[14] On the other hand, in EModE
shortened forms were commonly used alongside the longer ones
without differentiation in meaning, especially in poetry. Examples
are: *(a)gainst, (a)larum, (ap)parel, (de)stroy, (en)tice*.

§115 A vowel preceding the stress was often lost before another
vowel in EModE, as in *geography, geometry, georgics*, generally
pronounced [dʒɔ-] till *c*. 1800. The PresE pronunciation [dʒiˈɔ-] was
gaining ground according to Walker 1791 in *geography, geometry*.

---

[12] Also [fɔːtjuːn].
[13] By [ei] Ekwall means the 16th century diphthong developed from ME *ī* (as
in *die*) which becomes present-day [ai]; see §70 above.
[14] Fr. *étiquet*; prob. (O)F *estincelé* (ODEE).

Under this heading comes the loss of vowels before an initial vowel, e.g. in the definite article (cf. §196), in the particle *to* before infinitives (forms like *t'accuse, t'inspect* still occur in poetry in the 18th century), in pronouns (like *m'instructions* for *my i.* in Ben Jonson; cf. also §198). Here also belong *doff, don*, for *do off, do on*.

Loss of such a vowel before a consonant seldom occurs. [ə] is often weakly articulated today and may occasionally be lost, as in [præps] for *perhaps*.

§116   Loss of vowels in medial syllables.

Loss after a vowel: *creature, posy* (< *poesy*), sometimes in *diamond* [dai(ə)mənd]. In earlier ModE the loss is more widely evidenced. In EModE poetry words like *Beatrice, deity* were often disyllabic. According to Nares 1784 *violet* was pronounced *vi'let* except in poetry.

Loss of a vowel between consonants has frequently occurred. In some cases the vowel is no longer written, as in *comrade* (Fr. *camarade*), *curtsy* (from *courtesy*), *damsel* (Fr. *demoiselle*),[15] *fancy* (*fantasy*), *ordnance* (from *ordinance*); cf. on the other hand *business* [biznis], *colonel* [kə:nəl], *Gloucester, Leicester* [glɔstə, lestə], *venison* [venzn].[16] Often there is variation between forms with and without syncope, especially where the vowel precedes *l, n, r*, as in *average, definite, every, favourite, halfpenny, strawberry*; similar variation is recorded in EModE.

§117   Loss of a vowel in final syllables has rarely occurred in ModE. Here, no doubt, at least in part, belong cases like *can't, don't* for *can (do) not*.

In endings like *-ed, -es* etc., the vowel had usually been syncopated already in ME (cf. §§183, 187, 262). However, it is also sometimes pronounced in ModE.

-ed in verb-forms frequently counted as a syllable in EModE poetry; this ending was metrically syllabic in poetry even later. Notable is the pronunciation [id] in a few adjectives and participial adjectives like *dogged, naked, ragged, rugged, wicked, wretched, beloved, learned*.

-est in superlatives and verb-forms (like *thou takest*) is pronounced [ist]. Syncope is occasionally attested in EModE.

-eth in verb-forms (like *he loveth*) is always pronounced [iθ]. In EModE and ME the *e* was frequently silent in this ending; the regular [iθ] is to be explained by the fact that it was early replaced by *-es* in colloquial speech.

§118   If a vowel is lost before final [l, m, n] the consonant becomes

---

[15] OF *dam(e)isele*.

[16] Also [venizn] now, no doubt under the influence of the spelling.

syllabic, as in *battle* [batl][17] from ME *battaile* etc. Syllabic consonants are recorded with certainty from the 16th century onwards;
syllabic [r] seems also to have existed (in words like *father, labour*)
in the 16th century.

[n] after [r], however, did not become syllabic. From *iron*, ME
ĩren, came [aiərn], PresE [aiən]. Until *c.* 1800 words like *apron* (ME
napperon), *Catherine* were pronounced with [ərn]; PresE [eiprən,
kæθ(ə)rin]. *Byron* is said to have pronounced his name *Byrn*.

3. VOWEL > CONSONANT

§119   Unstressed [i] before a vowel has often become [j], as in
Indian, opinion, hideous [indjən, o'pinjən, hidjəs]. The change must
have taken place early since it is a prerequisite for such developments
as [sj] > [ʃ], [tj] > [tʃ], etc. (cf. §§155, 171, 174). Before stressed and
half-stressed vowels [i] has mostly been retained or re-introduced, as
in *association, paleography, physiology* [əsousi'eiʃn, pæli'ɔgrəfi,
fizi'ɔlədʒi], *appreciate* [ə'pri:ʃieit], etc. Also, where a too difficult
consonant-group would have resulted, [i] remained; e.g. in *equestrian,
glorious, obsequious*. Derivatives etc. like *easier, thirtieth* [i:ziə,
θə:tiiθ] depend on *easy, thirty* [i:zi, θə:ti], etc.

4. DEVELOPMENT OF NEW VOWELS

§120   After a long vowel or diphthong, especially ME ĩ, ū, ẽ, ọ,
ai, ẽu, before [r] there frequently developed in EModE or earlier a
glide-vowel [ə] which was often indicated by *e* or (more rarely) *a*, as
still in *bower, flower, friar* (ME *bour, flour, frēre*) etc.; cf. EModE
fier, hower and the like for *fire, hour* etc. This glide-vowel often counted
as a syllable in poetry (e.g. in Shakespeare). It is often mentioned by
the grammarians. PresE [ə] in words like *dear, poor* [diə, puə] probably stems, at least in part, from this glide-vowel (cf. also §130).
Today this [ə] combines with the original stem-vowel to make a
diphthong or triphthong, as in [iə, uə, aiə] etc.

---

[17] Presumably for [bætl].

III. The Consonants

Nasals

[m]

§121 The articulation of the bilabial nasal [m] has remained unchanged. Examples: *man* [mæn], *home* [houm].

After [z, θ, ð] final [m] has become syllabic; e.g. *schism* [sizm], *rhythm* [riθm, riðm].

[n]

§122 The articulation of the alveolar nasal [n] has remained unchanged. Examples: *no* [nou], *wine* [wain].

[n] before [g, k] tends to become [ŋ]. It is notable that the change has normally occurred only after a stressed or half-stressed vowel, e.g. in *concourse, congress, handkerchief, incubus, syncope*; rarely, on the other hand, after an unstressed vowel, as in *con'cur, in'crease* (vb).[18] This distinction is already recorded by Walker 1791 for example. *Nightingale*, however, has mostly [ŋ].[19] [n] in cases like *pancake, incommodious, 'increase* (sb.), etc., is due to the influence of *pan, in-* in cases like *inhuman* etc., *in'crease* (vb) etc.

Exceptional is the [m] that appears *c.* 1600 in *lime(tree)* (OE *lind*); Shakespeare has *line, -grove*.

§123 Loss of *n* occurred frequently in ME. Undoubted examples of ModE loss of *n* are rare. In late ME or EModE [n] dropped in *Leominster* [lemstə] < *-mister* (cf. EModE *-mister* for *-minster* in *Westminster* etc.), in earlier ModE *furmety* for *frumenty* (OF *frumentee*) and in *government* (in the 16th century and later often written *goverment* and still sometimes pronounced [gʌvəmənt] today[20]).

Loss of *n* after *m* is attested from the 16th century, as in *damn, hymn* (cf. EModE spellings like *hymme, solem*), from the ME period in *kiln*, nowadays [kil] or [kiln].[21] [n] was lost regularly only in final position, and also before a consonant, as in *solemnly*. Thus *damna-*

---

[18] EPD gives also (less commonly) [n] beside [ŋ] in *concourse, incubus*, and [n] as more common than [ŋ] in *concur, increase*.

[19] Exclusively [ŋ] now.

[20] Quite commonly in PresE.

[21] EPD notes that [kil] 'appears to be used only by those concerned with the working of kilns'.

tion, solemnity with [mn] go according to rule. Inflected forms like *condemning* with [m] have been influenced by *condemn* etc.

§124 Epenthesis of [n] after an unstressed medial vowel, as in *nightingale* (OE *nihtegale*), *harbinger* (<*herberger*), *messenger* (cf. *message*), *porringer* (cf. *porridge*), occurred for the most part in the ME period. First recorded in the ModE period is, e.g., *scavenger* for *scavager*. The epenthesis has evidently taken place at various times. The explanation of the phenomenon is disputed.

[ŋ]

§125 The articulation of the velar nasal has remained unchanged. Examples: *king* [kiŋ], *long* [lɔŋ].[22]

In popular London speech and in many dialects [ŋ] in the ending *-ing* has frequently become [n], and this pronunciation is found also in educated circles.[23] Examples: *morning* [mɔːnin], *doing* [duːin]. This pronunciation certainly existed in the 16th century, as is shown by spellings like *farden* for *farthing*, or *gudging* for *gudgeon*, etc. Orthoepists mention it from the 16th century onwards. It was probably more current in educated circles in earlier ModE than it is today. This pronunciation has become fully accepted in *midden* 'dung-hill' (ME *myddyng*).

LIQUIDS

[l]

§126 The articulation of the alveolar liquid [l] has probably remained unchanged in the ModE period. That late ME [l] had a hollow sound is shown by the fact that between [a, o] and [l] an [u] developed[24] (cf. §§35, 7; 88, 8). Examples of [l]: *live* [liv], *fill* [fil], *hall* [hɔːl].

§127 Loss of [l].

[l] is regularly lost between *au* or *ǭu* and *k* or *f, v, m, p, b*, e.g. in *talk, half, halve, alms, folk, Holborn* [tɔːk, haːf, haːv, aːmz, fouk,

---

[22] This statement, correct in itself, requires qualification in the light of §181 below; *ng* was originally pronounced [ŋg] in all positions, and [ŋ] became an independent phoneme only when the [g] was lost in various cases: until then it was an allophone of /n/. The change, in educated speech, was later than Ekwall supposed; it occurred about 1600 (Dobson, §§399, 412).

[23] Not nowadays.

[24] This certainly suggests a velar (or 'dark') *l* after back vowels and low front [a], but not necessarily elsewhere.

houbən]. The loss is mentioned by Mulcaster 1582. In a few words [l] has been restored, e.g. in *almighty, almost* under the influence of *all* (Ben Jonson writes *a'most*, and Nares 1784 still mentions the pronunciation *a-most*), in *almanack* [ɔːl-], *salve* [sælv], *scalp* [skælp], and others under the influence of the spelling.[25] *Palfrey* [pɔːlfri] is possibly to be explained by late syncope (ME *palefrai*).

More sporadically [l] is lost in other positions, e.g. before [m, n] as in *Chelmsford* [tʃemzfəd],[26] *Cholmondeley* [tʃʌmli], *Alnwick* [ænik], *Lincoln* [liŋkən], *shan't, won't*. The loss is attested from the 17th century at the latest. In addition, [l] has sometimes been lost in weakly stressed words, e.g. in *should, would* (though cf. §283 f.), *shalt* (*sha't* Wallis 1653), *wilt* (*woo't* in Shakespeare). Cf. also cases like EModE *gentman, gemman* for *gentleman, canstick* for *candlestick*, etc. *Fuzee, jaunty* (Fr. *fusil, gentil*) were borrowed after the loss of Fr. [l] (or its development to [j]). The pronunciation [kə:nəl] for *colonel* depends on the EModE form *coronel* (< Fr. *coronel*).

§128 Addition of [l].

In words of Fr. origin OF *au, ọu* from *al, ol* were in late ME and EModE frequently written with *al, aul, ol, oul* (evidently under the influence of the original Latin form). Thus *falcon, fault, so(u)ldier* etc. were written for ME *faucon, faute, soudiour* etc. Gradually this *l* began also to be pronounced. Already Bullokar 1580 and Gil 1621 and others attest a spoken [l] in words like *balm, fault*. For obvious[27] reasons [l] did not usually develop before [k] or labials, or if it did, became silent again. It is now silent for example in *balm, calm, salmon* etc., [baːm, sæmən] etc. In other positions it is nowadays usually pronounced, e.g. in *assault, fault, vault, Walter, herald, soldier* etc. But even in these, and in similar words, it was for a long time silent; right up to *c.* 1800 orthoepists give *l* as silent in *fault, vault,* and others. *Chaldron* and *solder* still vary [tʃɔːldrən, tʃaːdrən; sɔdə, sɔldə].[28] [l] is also often pronounced before *k* and labials in less common words like *halberd, Talbot*[29] [hælbəd, tɔːlbət], *falcon* [fɔː(l)kən]; on *almoner* and the like see §44.

[25] But see note 63 to §44 above.

[26] But now usually [tʃelmsfəd] under the influence of the spelling. EPD gives [tʃem-] as an 'old-fashioned local pronunciation'.

[27] Ekwall 'natürlichen'.

[28] [tʃaːdrən] appears to be obsolete in RP. Besides [sɔdə] in PresE also [sɔː-]; besides [sɔldə] also [səuldə].

[29] Also [hɔːl-] nowadays in *halberd*, and [tɔl-] in *Talbot*. Also [tæl-] in the place-name only.

Of a similar kind is the epenthesis of *l* in *realm* [relm] from EModE *reame* etc., OF *reaume*; the *l* is due to the influence of Lat. *regalis*.[30] *moult* [moult] from ME *mouten*, OE *mūtian* is odd.[31] *Bristol* (OE *Brycgstow*), mostly spelt *Bristol* in ModE (as today) after Lat. *Bristollum*, usually had a silent *l* till *c.* 1800.

[r]

§129 In EModE *r* was pronounced as a consonant in all positions, initially probably as a trill, medially and finally perhaps in the earlier period as a fricative, rather like PresE [r]. At least, Ben Jonson 1640 maintained that *r* medially and finally had a softer sound than initially.[32] PresE [r] is not a trill but an unrolled sound which can be described as an alveolar fricative. This was certainly the case *c.* 1800, since according to Batchelor 1809 'rough *r*' (i.e. rolled *r*) was a Scottish and Irish peculiarity only. PresE [r] occurs only before vowels. Examples: *ride* [raid], *merry* [meri], *Irish* [aiəriʃ].

§130 In other positions *r* is silent. It has been lost without trace after [aː, ɔː, ə], as in *far, cart, fur, turn, better, southern* [faː, kaːt, fəː, təːn, betə, sʌðən]. After [i, u, ɛ, ai, au] an [ə] is pronounced, as in *fear, poor, fire, hour* [fiə, puə, faiə, auə]; this [ə] derives at least in part from the EModE glide-sound [ə] which had developed before *r* (§120). After [ɔː] there is variation; examples: *more, court* [mɔː(ə), kɔː(ə)t].

It is not certain when the *r* in words like *far, fear* ceased to be pronounced as a consonant. Walker 1775 says that *haunch* is pronounced almost like *harnch*, and in 1791 he mentions the dropping of *r* in *card, lard* as a London peculiarity. Was *r* also silent after other vowels besides [aː]? We hear nothing about the loss of *r* from other 18th century teachers of pronunciation. This does not prove that [r] was pronounced, but at the most that *r* had some sound-value, e.g. [ə] or something similar. In present-day northern English and American, *r*, though often indeed silent, has affected the articulation of the preceding vowel so that it is a retroflex one (i.e. pronounced with the tongue-tip turned back). A similar pronunciation may have

---

[30] *-l-* forms occurred in OF, owing to the influence of OF *reiel* etc.

[31] Dobson suggests influence of *moulder, moulter* 'decay' (§174 n. 1). (OED has a different explanation.) '*mūtian*' should strictly be '*-mūtian*'.

[32] Jonson: 'more liquid'. But Dobson (§370 n.) regards this evidence as 'worthless' because taken from the French grammarian Ramée; see also Dobson, I, p. 326.

F

been current in the standard speech of the 18th century. The present
situation dates most probably from the first half of the 19th century.[33]

§131   Already in EModE (or even late ME) [r] was sporadically
lost, especially before [s], as in *dace* (the fish) (ME *darse*), *bass* (the
fish) (ME *bars*), *worsted* [wustid], *Worcester* [wustə]. [r] was lost
early in *forecastle* [fouksl], *Marlborough* [mɔːlbrə], as the quality of
the vowel shows.

§132   Occasionally an inorganic [r] has been added; e.g. in
cartridge (from the 17th century; from Fr. *cartouche*), perhaps under
the influence of *partridge* (a kind of shot),[34] *bridegroom* (from the
16th century, from OE *brȳdguma*), influenced by *groom*.

On the analogy of *better* [betə], but *better off* [betər ɔf] etc., an [r]
is often inserted in cases like *the idea of it*, *the India Office* (ai'diər ɔv,
indjər ɔfis]. This pronunciation is attested as a vulgar one from the
last decade of the 18th century.

FRICATIVES

[w]

§133   The bilabial fricative [w][35] occurs chiefly in Germanic
words, as in *wan*, *wind*, *window*, but also in Fr. and Lat. words like
war, *warden*, *quart*, *-er*, *quiet* etc. In a few cases [w] derives from OF
[u], as in *cuisse* [kwis] from Fr. *cuisse* (Lat. *coxa*), *choir* from AN
cuer (Lat. *chorum*), *quaint* from AN *cueint* (=Central Fr. *coint*), etc.
The articulation of the [w] has remained unchanged. Examples:
wind [wind], *choir* [kwaiə], *forward* [fɔːwəd].

§134   Loss of [w].

[w] has often been lost between a consonant and [uː, u]. After the
change of ǭ > [uː], and thus in late ME or EModE, is the loss of *w*
in *two*, *who* [tuː, huː][36], *sword* [sɔːd] < [suːrd]; loss is attested here by
16th century observers. In forms like *swore* [swɔːə], in EModE also
[suːr], *swum*, *swung*, the retention or restoration of the [w] is due to
the influence of *swear*, *swim* etc. *Swoon* [swuːn] has kept its [w]

---

[33] In fact the emergence of [ɛə] in *bare*, *scarce* etc., as a phoneme distinct from
[ei] < [eː] in *name* etc., which occurred in the late 18th century, shows that [r] had
already been lost; and there is other evidence before 1800.
[34] Though *partridge* in this sense is not recorded till over half a century later.
[35] It is not entirely satisfactory to describe [w] as a fricative, since the friction
is negligible except when [w] is partly or wholly devoiced (as, e.g., in *queen*).
[36] In fact loss of [w] in *two* and *who* occurs in ME; see the forms cited in OED.

probably under the influence of the spelling. In EModE it was sometimes written *soune, sound,* and pronounced with the diphthong in *now.*

[w] is also lost before [r], as in *wring* [riŋ],[37] *write* [rait]. The loss is attested by Hodges 1643, Price 1668, Cooper 1685, and others.

[w] is lost in the weak form of *will,* as in *I'll, you'll* [ail, juːl], etc.; the loss is attested in EModE. Perhaps the vowel was syncopated and [w] dropped before [l]; or the [l] really comes from the ME form [wul].

[w] is often lost after consonants at the beginning of a syllable following the main stress. In most of the following cases the loss is attested in the 16th and 17th centuries: *answer* [aːnsə] (cf. *ansere* etc. in the 16th century), *boatswain, coxswain* [bousn, kɔksn] (spellings like *boson, coxon* from the 17th century), *housewife* [hʌzif, hʌzwif[38]], cf. *huzzy Southwark,* [sʌðək], names in *-wich, -wick,* like *Greenwich, Berwick* [grinidʒ, berik] (loss of *w* recorded by Elphinston 1765), and others. Often the [w] has been restored under the influence of the spelling or is in process of being so. Thus *boatswain, coxswain* are also pronounced [boutswein, kɔkswein], *housewife* mostly [hauswaif], *Ipswich* [ipswitʃ]. In earlier ModE *w* was often silent where it is now pronounced; e.g. in words in *-ward,* like *awkward, forward, northward;* today [ɔːkwəd] etc., but *southward* [sʌðəd] beside [sauθwəd].[39]

§135 Addition of [w].

In a number of Fr. loanwords [k, g] were written as *qu, gu* in ME and ModE after the Fr. forms. Gradually this *u* began to be pronounced as [w]. In EModE *qu* and *gu* were frequently pronounced [k, g], e.g. in the following words: *quote* (also written *cote*), *quotidian, banquet, equipage, marquis, language.* The old pronunciation is still often recorded in the 18th century; Elphinston 1765 has, e.g., [k] in *banquet, equipage, harlequin, marquis.* Today [kw, gw] have for the most part prevailed (except in the words mentioned below), e.g. in *conquest, equal, languid, liquid.* [k, g] are still pronounced in a few words, especially in late loanwords, e.g. *bouquet, coquette, liquor, masquerade, piquant, piquet. Harlequin, languor, quoit* still vary.[40]

---

[37] Ekwall [riŋ].
[38] See also below, and note 2 to §110.
[39] [sʌðəd] appears to be restricted now to nautical use.
[40] EPD only [kw] in *harlequin,* only [g] in *languor.*

[hw]

§136   OE *hw* (in *hwæt* etc.) was usually written *wh* already in ME, which probably indicates a change to a voiceless [w]. We shall indicate this voiceless [w] by [hw].

In EModE *w* and *wh* were well kept apart in the spelling, and orthoepists make a distinction between the sounds in *wide* and *what*. Jones 1701 is the first[41] to give *wat, wen* as occasional pronunciations for *what, when*. Towards the end of the 18th century [hw] fell together with [w] in the standard language, and [w] is today the usual pronunciation of *wh* in southern English; thus, *what* [wɔt], *when* [wen]. In northern English [hw] is used regularly, and even in southern English it is frequently used, or at least aimed at, partly because of the influence of the schools.[42]

[f]

§137   The articulation of the voiceless labio-dental fricative [f] has remained unchanged. Examples: *feed* [fiːd], *stiff* [stif].

[f] has become [v] in the often unemphatic *of* [ɔv, əv]; [v] is attested by Hart 1569, who, however, as also Walker 1791, has [f] in *thereof*. *If*, PresE [if], was in earlier ModE often pronounced [iv]. [v] is historically correct in *nephew, Stephen* [nevju, stiːvən]; cf. Fr. *neveu*, AN *Esteven*, etc.

Frequent [p] for *ph* [f] in *diphtheria, diphthong, naphtha* no doubt comes from the French.

[f] has been sporadically lost, e.g. in *huzzy* from *huzwif* (*housewife*), perhaps influenced by pet-names in *-y*. Already in ME [f] had been lost in *of* (EModE often *o'*, still in use in *o'clock*), *halfpenny*. The initial group *phth-*, as in *phthisis, phthisic*, is often pronounced [t] or [θ]; *phthisic* [tizik] was, in fact, borrowed from OF. *tisique*.

[v]

§138   The articulation of the voiced labio-dental fricative [v] has remained unchanged. Examples: *vine* [vain], *live* [liv].

[v] has occasionally become [f]. [f] in *lieutenant* [lef-, lev-] goes

---

[41] There is in fact some earlier evidence; see Dobson, §414.

[42] [hw-] is used less frequently now than formerly, and it is doubtful if many schools now encourage it.

back to ME times, *sheriff* for ME *schirreve* (cf. the by-form *shrieve*) is probably modelled on *bailiff*. *Belief* (ME *ilẹve*), *proof* (cf. Fr. *épreuve*[43]), are analogical remodellings on *believe, prove* (after *strife* : *strive* etc.).[44]

[v] disappeared in EModE before labial consonants, as in *fivepence*, sometimes written *fippence* in EModE, *gimme* for *give me*, *pament* for *pavement*, *twelmonth* for *twelvemonth* etc. Today *v* is pronounced in these cases.

Already in ME the loss had taken place in words like *even, ever, over*. Forms like *e'en, e'er, o'er* are nowadays poetic, but were in general use in EModE. *Sevennight* [senit] is obsolete.

[θ]

§139 The voiceless post-dental fricative [θ] represents OE (ON) þ [θ] in initial and final position and when geminated; e.g. *thing, thrive, death* (OE *dēaþ*),[45] *forth, path, moth* (OE *moþþe*); AN [θ] in *faith*. Derivatives mostly follow the original word, e.g. *deathly, mouthful, northward* [θ]; cf. however, §141. On plurals like *baths* cf. §188. On [θ] from [ð] and [t], see §§142, 170.

§140 The articulation of the [θ] has remained unchanged. Examples: *thing* [θiŋ],[46] *moth* [mɔθ].

[θ] has become [ð] in the unemphatic *with*, nowadays [wið], rarely [wiθ]. The form [wið] is attested by Hart 1569, who also has [ð] in *doth, saith*. [θ] has occasionally become [ð] in *rhythm* [riθm, riðm].[47]

[θ] is sometimes silent in *northwest, southwester* etc., often written *nor'west, sou'wester* etc. from the 16th century onwards; in *months* [mʌn(θ)s], *sixths* [siksθs, siks], etc.

[ð]

§141 The voiced post-dental fricative [ð] represents:
1. OE (ON) þ [ð] medially between voiced sounds, as in *bathe* (OE *baþian*), *scythe* (OE *sigþe*), *seethe, smooth, brother, farthing; northern, southern, Southwark, worthy*.
2. OE þ [θ] initially in pronominal words like *the, that, then, there* etc., in which [θ] became [ð] in ME.

---

[43] Cf. OF *prueve* etc.
[44] ODEE regards these as cases of [v] > [f] after loss of the final vowel.
[45] Ekwall: *deaþ*.
[46] Ekwall: [þing].
[47] In fact [ð] is commoner than [θ] in *rhythm*; so OED in 1914 and EPD.

§142 The articulation has remained unchanged. Examples: *bathe* [beið], *Southwark* [sʌðək], *that* [ðæt, ðət].

Final [ð] became [θ] in late ME or EModE, regularly after consonants, as in *earth* [ə:θ], *fourth, ninth* (OE *eorþe, fēorþa, nigoþa*), and frequently after a vowel, as in *Bath* (ME *Bāþe*), *froth* (ME *frōþe*), *-mouth* as in *Portsmouth* (OE *-mūþa*), *pith* (OE *piþa*), [ba:θ, frɔθ, -məθ, piθ]. Perhaps the change took place after a short (or shortened) vowel; the above words had a short vowel in EModE. *Beneath, both* [bini:θ, bouθ] are perhaps mixed forms of EModE [-ne:ð, bo:ð] and [-neθ, bɔθ]. In *bequeath, booth*, occasional [θ][48] is probably due to the influence of the spelling; [leiθəm], the pronunciation of the name *Latham* (ME *Lathum* with [ð])[49]) is to be explained in the same way. The history of words like *health, truth, youth*, all with [θ], *betroth* [bi'trɔþ,[50] -trouð] is unclear.[51]

[ð] is sometimes silent in *clothes* [klou(ð)z].[52]

In ME [ð] before (*e*)*l*, (*e*)*r* often became [d]; this has prevailed in *burden*,[53] *fiddle, murder, rudder*,[54] and others. Spellings like *burthen, murther* were extremely common in earlier ModE; *burthen* in the sense of 'tonnage' is in fact still in use. Exceptional is *afford* for ME *aforthe*.[55] The reverse change of [d] to [ð] also took place in ME; [ð] derives from [d] in *father, hither, mother, weather*, and others.[56]

[s], [z]

§143 The articulation of the alveolar fricatives [s, z] has remained unchanged in the ModE period.

1. The distribution of [s] and [z]. We confine ourselves here to native (and Scandinavian) and Fr. and Lat. words.

(a) Native (and Scandinavian) words

§144 OE *s* was voiceless in initial and final position, and medially in the neighbourhood of a voiceless sound; it was voiced medially

---

[48] Now only [ð].

[49] EPD: '*Generally* 'leiθəm *in S. of England; always* 'leiðəm *in N.*'

[50] No longer [ɔ] in this word.

[51] On this whole subject see Dobson, §368.

[52] EPD gives [kləuz] as 'old-fashioned'.

[53] But note this is before (*e*)*n*.

[54] Different cases are placed together here. On *fiddle* etc. see Luick, §724 (2), on *rudder* (and *spider*) §725.

[55] OED and ODEE compare *d* in *burden*, though *–d–* forms are late in *afford* (16th century).

[56] Note that in these the consonant is preceded by a vowel, in contrast to *burden, murder, afford*.

between voiced sounds except when beginning an element of a compound word where the element had preserved a distinct meaning. Scandinavian loanwords apparently followed the same rule. The OE distribution was retained in ME and ModE; the [z] that appeared in final position as a result of the loss of final -*e* thus remained [z]. [s] is therefore regular in *sea, goose* (OE *gōs*), *house* (OE *hūs*), *louse, horse*; *answer* (OE *andswerian*), *beside, forsake, groundsel* (OE *grundeswelge*), *handsome* etc.; [z] in *busy, dizzy, hazel, huzzy, Osmond*; *cleanse* (OE *clǣnsian*), *choose* (OE *cēosan*), *freeze, rise, rouse, wheeze* etc.

§145 There are exceptions, however. The alternation of [s] and [z] in paradigms has for the most part been set aside, in favour of [s] in cases like *fleece, horse*, or of [z] as in *furze*. Cf. also §§188, 209. Derivatives mostly follow the original word; e.g. *loosely* with [s] after *loose*, etc. But the regular alternation has sometimes been preserved; thus *house, mouse* have [s] as sbs. but [z] as vbs;[57] *lousy* has [z], *louse* [s].

In ME, final [s] after an unstressed vowel became [z], as in *fishes* [fiʃiz], *as, is, his, was*. The same change perhaps occurred in *eaves, Thames* [iːvz, temz] from OE *efes, Temes*, and certainly did so in Fr. names like *Charles, James*. Unusual is the [s] in *else, hence, once, twice* etc., from ME *elles, hennes* etc.[58]

(b) Fr. and Lat. words

§146 English [s] represents as a rule Fr. or Lat. [s], [z] Fr. or Lat. [z].

In French, [s] is indicated by *s, c, ç, ss, sc, t*; [z] chiefly by *s, z*. Intervocalic *s* almost always indicates [z], *s* before or after consonants almost always [s]. Final silent *s* was probably voiceless before it became silent.

[s] represents Fr. [s] in, e.g., *sign, counsel* (Fr. *conseil*), *person, chase* (Fr. *chasse*), *lease* (Fr. *laisser*), *mason* (Fr. *maçon*), *obeisance*, (Fr. *obéissance*), *sausage* (Fr. *saucisse*); Fr. silent *s* in *abuse, case, course, sense,*[59] *tense* (Fr. *abus, cas, cours, sens, temps*).

---

[57] Also [maus] now besides [mauz].

[58] These words have [s] because of early contraction of the ending -*es* to -*s*, before the date when final [s] became [z] after an unstressed vowel. In EModE some of them had [z] as well as [s]; cf. Dobson, §363 (i).

[59] In fact from Lat. *sensus*. (Note, however, that these Mod. Fr. forms are not to be taken as etymologies.)

[z] represents Fr. [z] in *zeal* (Fr. *zèle*),[60] *cousin, damsel* (Fr. *demoiselle*), *abuse* (vb) (Fr. *abuser*), *ease* (Fr. *aise*), *physic, pleasant, reason, scissors* (cf. Fr. *ciseaux*), *tansy* (the herb) (Fr. *tanaisie*), *Lisbon* (Fr. *Lisbonne*), etc.

§147 There is variation in French between [s] and [z] after prefixes like *de-, pre-, re-*, and in the prefixes *des-, trans-*. In conformity with French, English usually has [z], as in *deserve, desire, present, preserve, reserve, resume*. In French, [s] occurs where the connexion with the original word is felt to be present; for this reason English has [s] in *presentiment, resource*[61] (Fr. *pressentiment, ressource*) and others. The same tendency has become noticeable in English also. *Dis-* is often [dis-] where the uncompounded verb or noun is a living one; thus, e.g., in *disarm, -order, -own* (but [z] in *disaster, disease*). *Dishonour, -honest* vary; their French equivalents have [z]. In the 18th century, [z] was also frequently used in *disable, -arm* etc.; it is still heard occasionally.

§148 Latin loanwords have predominantly [s]. Examples: *asylum, desolate, desultory, episode,*[62] *parasite, prosody; morose* etc.; *basis, thesis* etc. A few early loanwords have [z], like *Caesar, miser*; perhaps intervocalic *s* was pronounced [z] in the medieval school-pronunciation of Latin.[63] In ModE school-pronunciation Lat. *s* is pronounced [s] except in isolated cases, such as in the ending *-es* [iːz], e.g. *Hercules*, finally after a consonant (*mons, pons* etc.), and sometimes before endings like *-ia, -ium* etc. In conformity with this, [z] is pronounced in English words like *dives, Hercules, series* (here [z] is attested with certainty from the 18th century), *lens, Mars; ambrosia, aphasia, euphrasia* (in these words [z] is attested from the 18th century onwards), *Elysian, Elysium* (cf. spellings like *Elyzian* from the 16th century on).

§149 The rules given above are sometimes broken through analogy.

The consistent [s] in endings like *-osity* (*curiosity, generosity* etc.), *-sory* (*illusory* etc.; however, [z] in *advisory, divisory*), *-sive* (as in *decisive*), which occur in both Lat. and Fr. words and thus ought to have partly [z], partly [s], is explained by the generalization of Lat. [s]. Similarly, [z] in endings like *-sible* (*visible* etc.), *-site* (as in

---

[60] LLat. *zēlus*.
[61] But also now [z] in both words.
[62] This is from Greek.
[63] It was; in 1617 Robinson gives [z] in *imposui, expositrix*.

opposite etc.), *-sition* (as in *opposition*) is due to the generalization of Fr. [z]. [s] may be due to Lat. influence in words like *chrysolite, philosopher, philosophy, presage*, which are probably originally Fr. loanwords.[64]

Similar suffixes have influenced each other. Thus we expect [z] in some words with *-son* (like *comparison, garrison, orison, venison*, from Fr. *comparaison* etc.), [s] in others (like *caparison, benison, unison*, from Fr. *caparaçon, benisson, unisson*).[65] Through analogy [s] has sometimes spread into the first group, [z] into the second. Statements about these words in the 18th century vary considerably. Today [s] prevails except in *orison, venison; unison* has [s] and [z].[66]

The sb.-ending *-sy* is mostly pronounced [si], as in *courtesy, heresy, jealousy, poesy*;[67] the expected [z] is given by Bullokar 1580 in *jealousy*, by Gil 1621 in *courtesy*. Today we have [z] in *palsy, posy, tansy*, where it is to be expected, and in *pansy, quinsy*, where we would expect [s](< Fr. *pensée*, Lat. *quinancia*[68]). *Pansy* has been influenced by *tansy, quinsy* by *frenzy, palsy*.[69] In *courtesy* etc. [s] is probably due to the influence of words in *-cy* (like *privacy, secrecy*). Lat. forms like *haeresis, poësis*, may also have contributed.

Related words have influenced one another. *Purpose* (vb) should have [z], but has [s] after the sb. *purpose; practice* (sb.) with [s] has influenced *practise* (vb).

(c) Pronunciation of *x*

§150   Initially *x* is pronounced [z], e.g. *Xerxes, Xenophon*. [z] is attested here with certainty from the 18th century (Walker 1791, etc.). It derives, perhaps, from earlier Fr. [z], or comes from [gz], the present Fr. pronunciation of initial *x*. Elphinston 1765 transcribes *Xerxes* as *Gzercses*.

---

[64] ODEE derives from Lat. without qualification, except for *presage*, which is given as 'chiefly' from Fr. *présage*, but in Gower immediately from its Lat. source.

[65] Again, these should not be taken as exact etymologies; Ekwall is no doubt citing ModF forms as more expressive of the [s]/[z] distinction. ODEE derives *unison* from (O)F *unison* 'or LateL. *ūnisonus*'. Dobson, §356 n. 4, explains [s] here as due to the Lat. word.

[66] So also now *benison*.

[67] Now only [z] in *poesy*.

[68] OF *quinencie*.

[69] Dobson (§356 n. 4) observes that Ekwall 'does not allow sufficiently ... for the tendency of [s] to become [z] after voiced consonants, which certainly affects *pansy* and *quinsy*'.

Final *x* is always [ks], as in *axe, sex*.

Medially, *x* before a consonant and silent *c* is pronounced [ks], as in *explain, exceed*; before a stressed vowel mostly [gz], before an unstressed one mostly [ks]. Thus [gz] in *Alexander, anxiety, exalt, examine, example, exist, exult* etc.; [ks], however, in *axiom, exercise, execute, exodus* etc. Words like *exhibit, exhaust* (with silent *h*) have [gz]; the less common *exhale* is pronounced [ig'zeil][70] or [eks'heil]. We find [ks] sometimes before a stressed vowel in learned words like *ex'animate, ex'ude, lux'ation*, and (after '*execute* etc.), in *ex'ecutive, ex'ecutor*, though also [gz]. Before an unstressed vowel [gz] occurs instead of [ks] in derivatives like *exaltation, exultation*. *Exile* is pronounced ['eksail, 'egzail]; in the 18th century the sb. was pronounced ['eksail], the vb [eg'zail].

§151 The current distribution of [gz] and [ks] is recorded with unimportant exceptions by the orthoepists of the latter half of the 18th century. It is probably a great deal older. [gz] is usually explained as due to a sound-change of [ks] to [gz] before a stressed vowel, and a parallel has been seen between this sound-change and so-called Verner's Law. It should be noted, however, that the change often fails to take place, e.g. in words like *accept, exceed, except* etc., and also that an alternation of [ks] and [gz] occurs in French, from which the English one can hardly be dissociated out of hand. In French, [ks] is invariable in words like *excès, excepter, accepter*; so is [gz] in the case of *ex-* before a vowel (as in *exemple, exister*), and silent *h* (as in *exhiber*). English [gz] in fact corresponds in the great majority of cases to French [gz]. On the other hand, English [ks] derives in most cases from French, Latin, or OE [ks]. At all events, an English sound-change of [ks] > [gz] needs to be assumed only in a few isolated cases.[71]

2. ModE changes affecting [s, z].

§152 [z] has occasionally become [s] in the neighbourhood of voiceless sounds, as in [ist] for *is it*, [its] for *it is*, [juːst] for *used (to)* 'was accustomed' (on the other hand *used* 'made use of' is [juːzd]; Nares 1784 mentions this distinction).

§153 Before voiced consonants, especially [l, m], [s] has not uncommonly become [z]. Examples: *mistletoe* [mizl-, misl-], *muslin* [mʌzlin] from Fr. *mousseline, Wesley* < *Westley*; *prism, schism, enthusiasm* etc. [prizm] etc. (already Gil 1621 has [z] in *sophism*);

[70] EPD [eg'-].
[71] Probably only in *anxiety*; see Dobson, §359.

cosmic, dismal, Mesmer etc. However, [z] before [m] may derive, at least in part, from French. Before [b] we have [z] in *gooseberry, raspberry, wristband* [riz-,[72] ris-]; it is doubtful whether [z] is of English origin in, e.g., *Lesbian*, earlier *presbyter* (Nares 1784), *Sophonisba* (Elphinston 1765), or in PresE *Bosnia*.

§154 [s] has also become [z] in a few cases before a vowel with main stress, namely in *dessert, discern*,[73] *dissolve, possess, resemble* (Fr. *ressembler*), *resent* (Fr. *ressentir*); *absolve, observe*, perhaps in *museum, philosophic*.[74] [z] is attested in the 18th century (Nares 1784, Walker 1791, etc.). *Hussar* [hu'zaː] probably comes from German *Husar*.[75] [z] has been explained as due to a sound-change before a stressed vowel, and again Verner's Law has been compared. However, [s] in this position has not normally become [z], and in fact has remained not only where written *sc, c, ss* etc. (*descend, decide, precise, assault, assume*), but also where written *s*, as in *beside, presage, research, resource*[76] etc. Accordingly there can scarcely be any question of a law, but at most a tendency for [s] to become [z] before a vowel with main stress, which can be connected with the fact that it is just here (and especially after *de-, re-* etc., and in *dis-*) that [z] frequently occurs. *Absolve, observe* may be compared with *gooseberry* etc. *Philosophic* may have preserved an older [z], which in *philosopher* etc. was exchanged for [s] (cf. §149).

§155 [sj] has frequently become [ʃ], [zj] > [ʒ].

This change has often taken place in words ending in *-ia, -iable, -ian, -ion* etc., in which [i] has become [j], e.g. in cases like *special, nation*. The change is attested by Hodges 1644,[77] but spellings like *marshal* for *martial* appear already in the 16th century. Before an unstressed vowel [ʃ, ʒ] is in general the accepted pronunciation today, e.g. in *sociable, special, Egyptian, conscience, portion, vision* etc., [souʃəbl, viʒən] etc. Before a stressed or half-stressed vowel this pronunciation is frequently recorded in the 17th and 18th centuries. Cooper 1685 has [ʃ, ʒ] for *si, ci* in *associate, enthusiasm, ecclesiastical*

---

[72] EPD describes the [z] forms as 'old-fashioned'.
[73] [s] is now more usual in *discern*.
[74] [s] is more usual now in *philosophic*.
[75] OED derives *hussar* directly from Magyar *huszar*, and its early quotations confirm this. But the modern English pronunciation may have been influenced by German, as Ekwall suggests.
[76] Now also with [z].
[77] And earlier by Robinson (1617).

etc.; similarly Sheridan still in 1780. Usually in the second half of the 18th century, instead of [ʃ, ʒ] in such cases, a compromise-form between [ʃ, ʒ] and [si, zi] or [sj, zj] is given, namely [ʃi, ʒi].[78] Walker 1791 has this pronunciation in, e.g., *association, conscientious, partiality, acacia, ambrosia, nuncio* etc. In words of this kind [ʃj, ʒj] or [ʃi, ʒi] is still the most usual pronunciation; however, there is a tendency to use [sj, zj] or [si, zi] instead of [ʃj] etc., which is no doubt due to the influence of the spelling. Thus *ecclesiastic, enthusiasm, physiology* and others, which have [ʒi] in Walker, are now pronounced with [zi]. Variation occurs, for example, in words in *-ciation* (*pronunciation* mostly [si], *association* and others [si, ʃi]), *-cia, -sia*, such as *acacia, ambrosia* [-ʃə, -ʒə; -ʃjə, -ʒjə; -sjə, -zjə] and others. Also in words like *nauseate, omniscience, transient, brazier, grazier, hosier* we find [ʃi, ʒi] and [si, zi] etc. *Parisian* is mostly [pə'rizjən].[79]

§156   Rather later, e.g. in Cooper 1685 etc., [ʃ, ʒ] is evidenced in words like *usual, measure*, where [s, z] have been merged with the first element of the diphthong [iu], whence [juː]. It is to be noted that in words like *censure, measure*, EModE [iu] had commonly become [ə]; these words were often pronounced [sensər, mezər] etc. into the 18th century. The pronunciation [ʃ, ʒ] is the usual one today in common words like *censure, measure, pressure, luxury, usual* etc. [senʃə, meʒə] etc. In less familiar words [sj, zj] or even [ʃj, ʒj] is now often used, evidently under the influence of the spelling. Though Walker 1791 gives [ʃ] in, e.g., *insular, peninsular*, [sj] is now the accepted pronunciation. There is variation in a few words, such as *casual, visual, issue* [kæʒ(j)uəl, kæzjuəl; iʃu,[80] iʃju, isju], etc.

Before a stressed vowel [sj] has become [ʃ] only in *sugar, sure* and their derivatives; [zj] has become [ʒ] in *luxurious* etc. [ʃugə, ʃuə, lʌg'ʒuəriəs]. In earlier ModE, [ʃ] is also attested in other words, like *sue, suet* etc.

This change must have taken place already in the 16th century; Shakespeare has a play on words between *suitor* and *shooter* in *Love's Labour's Lost*. On *sewer*, see §86.

[78] For earlier examples, and a different explanation, see Dobson, I, p. 210, and II, §§276, 433.
[79] There has been an increasing tendency recently to use [s, z] in these and similar words, chiefly, no doubt, under the influence of the spelling. E.g., *pronunciation* has only [s] in EPD, and [s, z] are commoner than [ʃ, ʒ] in the other words.
[80] Now more correctly [iʃuː]; EPD does not record [iʃu].

[ʃ]

§157 [ʃ] derives chiefly from OE *sc*, e.g. in *shake, fish*; less commonly from Fr. palatalized *s* (<Lat. *sk, stj* etc.), as in *finish* (cf. Lat. *-isco*), *anguish* (Fr. *angoisse*, Lat. *angustia*), *cushion, fashion, issue* (ME *isshue* etc., cf. Lat. *exire*), *cash* (Fr. *caisse*, Lat. *capsa*), etc.[81] In late loanwords [ʃ] frequently represents Fr. [ʃ] < [tʃ], e.g. in *champagne, charade, Charlotte, chauffeur* etc. In *Gresham, Lewisham* etc. (with the suffix *-ham*), [ʃ] is a spelling-pronunciation. On [ʃ] < [sj] see §§155 f.

The articulation of [ʃ] has remained unchanged. Examples: *ash* [æʃ], *shoe* [ʃuː], *fashion* [fæʃən].

[tʃ]

§158 The articulation of the affricate [tʃ] has remained unchanged. Examples: *child* [tʃaild], *witch* [witʃ], etc. On [tʃ] < [tj] see §171.

After [l, n], [tʃ] has often become [ʃ], as in *belch, bench* [belʃ, benʃ] etc. [ʃ] is attested from the 16th century onwards. The older pronunciation [tʃ] is still in use, however; in *Manchester, Winchester*, it is general, evidently owing to the influence of *Chester, Dorchester* etc.[82]

In unstressed syllables [tʃ] has often become [dʒ], as in *cabbage* (Fr. *caboche*), *cartridge* (Fr. *cartouche*), *partridge* (ME *pertriche*), *-wich* as in *Harwich* [hæridʒ], *spinach* [spinidʒ]. [dʒ] is recorded in EModE (in *knowledge, ostrich* [ɔstridʒ][83] already in ME). *Ipswich* is mostly [ipswitʃ].[84] In *ajar* (ME, EModE *on char*) the change has taken place before a stressed vowel.

[ʒ]

§159 The voiced fricative [ʒ] makes its first appearance in the ModE period, deriving either from [zj] as in *measure* [meʒə] etc. (cf. §§155 f.), or from Fr. [ʒ], as in *prestige, rouge* [preˈstiːʒ, ruːʒ].

---

[81] Again, Ekwall is presumably not aiming to give us the exact etymologies, but ModFr equivalents. E.g. *anguish* is in fact from OF *anguisse*.
[82] The syllable division is sufficient reason for the difference from *bench*.
[83] But usually [ɔstritʃ] now.
[84] [tʃ] only now.

[dʒ]

§160 The articulation of the affricate [dʒ] has remained un-changed. Examples: *joy* [dʒoi], *rage* [reidʒ], *bridge* [bridʒ]. On [dʒ] < [dj] cf. §174.

[dʒ] has occasionally become [ʒ] after [l, n], as in *bilge*,[85] *angel*, *strange* etc. [bil(d)ʒ, ein(d)ʒəl, strein(d)ʒ].

[ç]

§161 The voiceless palatal fricative (the '*ich*-sound')[86] was common in OE and ME before *t* and finally. In ME it was mostly written *gh*, as in *bright*, *eight*, *high*, and this has remained in con-temporary orthography. The [ç] was still pronounced, in certain circles at least, in the 16th century, as the statements of the orthoe-pists (Hart 1569 etc.) show. It was apparently completely lost in the 17th century.[87] The fact that [ç] had already begun to disappear in the 16th century or earlier is shown by inverted spellings like *delight*, *kight* (ME *delit*, *kite*).[88]

The loss occurred gradually. [i] before the weakened [ç] was lengthened in late ME; PresE *fight* [fait] goes back to late ME [fiːçt], or even [fiːt].[89]

[j]

§162 The articulation of the voiced palatal fricative[90] [j] has apparently remained unchanged in ModE. The English [j] is articu-lated less close than the north German one and is often described as a semi-vowel. [j] often comes from [i], as in *million*, *opinion*, or *due*, *few* (cf. §§62 ff.). On [s, z, t, d] + [j] > [ʃ, ʒ, tʃ, dʒ] see §§155 f., 171, 174.

---

[85] Only [bildʒ] now.

[86] Ekwall means, of course, the sound used in German *ich*.

[87] But not till *c.* 1650, though the loss was common from early in the century.

[88] There is some evidence for analogical [ç] in *delight*, *kite*, and *spright* (see Dobson, §141.)

[89] It is more accurate to say that from later ME onwards there were two main pronunciations, [iç] with retained [ç] and short [i], and [iː] (identical with ME *i*) which became PresE [ai]; the latter gradually drove out the former. There is also evidence of a third pronunciation, [iːç] > [əiç] (as assumed by Ekwall), but it was less common. See Dobson, §§140–3.

[90] Cf. Ekwall's description of [w]. Friction is sometimes, but not always, audible in [j], depending on the phonetic context. See Gimson, §§208–10.

[j] is sometimes lost before [i], as in *harkee, lookee* for *hark ye, look ye* (in use in the 18th and 19th centuries), and after [dʒ] in *legion* [liːdʒən] etc.

[x]

§163 The voiceless velar fricative was common in OE and ME, especially before *t* and finally. In ME it was mostly written *gh*, and this has survived in the spelling, as in *bought, dough*. In the 16th century [x] was still to some extent pronounced, as is shown by the evidence of grammarians (Hart 1569 etc.). In the 17th century it was either silent or had become [f]. Today the *gh* is silent in *bought, brought* etc., *bough, daughter, dough, plough, slaughter, slough* 'pool', *through* and others.

The change of [x] to [f] is to be explained by the fact that [x] was pronounced with lip-rounding; cf. ME spellings like *lauhwen* = *laugh*, and the change of [ax, ox] to [aux, oux], §§35, 4; 88, 6. Already in ME [x] had become [f] in *dwarf* (OE *dweorh*). As a result of the ModE change to [f], which seems to have taken place in the 16th century,[91] *au, ōu, ū* became *a, o, u*, which have subsequently developed like ME *a, o, u*. [f] is pronounced today in *chough, cough, draught, enough, rough, slough* 'skin', *tough, trough* [tʃʌf, kɔf, draːft, i'nʌf, rʌf, slʌf, tʌf, trɔf] and others.

In earlier ModE [f] is often attested in words which now do not have it, e.g. in *daughter* (Butler 1633, Daines 1640 etc.), *bought* etc. (Price 1668 etc.), and vice-versa there was loss in words which now have [f]. Apparently we have to suppose two developments of [x]. The PresE distribution is the result of a long struggle between the two. Forms like *bough, dough* [bau, dou] may in part derive from ME disyllabic forms (e.g. ME *bowes* (pl.) from OE *bōgas*, beside *bough* from OE *bōh*).

A ME change of [x] to [k] occurs in *hough* [hɔk] from OE *hōh*, EModE *hekfer* (= *heifer*) for OE *hēahfore*. [k] in *hock* (German *Hochheimer*) is a substitution for German [x].

[h]

§164 The articulation of the aspirate [h] has remained un-

---

[91] Late ME rather; [f] here seems to have been adopted into the standard language from dialectal or vulgar speech (see Dobson, §371).

changed. It is heard only before vowels and [j]. Examples: *hat* [hæt], *behold* [bi'hould], *hew* [hju:].

§165   Loss of [h].

Initially before a vowel [h] is dropped in many dialects and in popular London speech. Already Walker 1791 warns against the dropping of initial [h].

Medially before a stressed vowel [h] is often silent in *perhaps* [pə'ræps] or [pə'hæps]. *Exhibit, exhort* [ig'zibit, ig'zɔ:t], etc., have been taken over from French with silent *h*. Otherwise [h] is mostly pronounced, as in *apprehend, Behemoth, dishearten* etc.

[h] is often silent before a weakly stressed vowel, e.g. in words like *he'reditary, his'torical*, as a result of which the indefinite article often has the form [æn, ən] before it, and the definite article the form [ði]. In addition, *h* is often silent in weakly-stressed words like *he, him, his, her, have* etc. Loss of [h] here is frequently attested from the ME period on. OE *hit* had commonly become *it* already in ME; in ModE *hit* is very rare.[92]

Still commoner is loss before a vowel following the stress. Examples: *Graham* [greiəm], *vehement, vehicle* etc.; *Chatham, Pelham*, and the like, *forehead*,[93] *shepherd, Stanhope* etc. But *h* is for the most part pronounced in compounds where the connexion between the two words is felt to be a living one, as in *Bathurst*,[94] *boathouse, playhouse, somehow* etc.; also in derivatives like *livelihood, manhood*. In earlier ModE loss of *h* is recorded in these cases also.

§166   Addition of [h].

In OF, *h-* in words of Lat. origin was silent, although it was often retained in the spelling. In English, no [h] was pronounced in words of this sort from the outset, as is shown by spellings. In the 16th century *abite, ipocrite, onest, yperbole* etc., were still written for *habit* etc. It soon became the rule, however, to write the *h-*, though *able, arbour, ostler* (from Lat. *habilis* etc.), continue to be written thus. Gradually this *h-* began to be pronounced, and today initial *h-* (except in the cases mentioned in §165) is only silent in the common words *heir, -ess, honest, honour* (with derivatives), *hour*, and sometimes before [ju:] as in *human, humour*.[95] In the 18th century *h-* was

---

[92] Though there are two apparent examples as late as the 1623 folio of Shakespeare (Onions, *Shakespeare Glossary*, under *hit*).

[93] But forms with [h] (under the influence of the spelling) are now very common.

[94] EPD gives only [bæθə(:)st]. Ekwall's comment assumes [bæthə(:)st].

[95] EPD gives only [hj-] in *human*, and describes [ju:-] in *humour* as old-fashioned.

silent in other words: e.g. according to Nares 1784 in *herb, hospital, humble*; according to Elphinston 1790 in these and in *heritage, homage, Humphrey*.

PLOSIVES

[p]

§167 The articulation of the voiceless bilabial plosive [p] has remained unchanged. Examples: *pin* [pin], *hope* [houp].

[p] is lost before [b] in *cupboard, raspberry* [kʌbəd, raːzbəri]; spellings like *cobbord, rasberry*, are found in the 16th century. The intrusive [p] that appeared in the ME period between [m] and [s, t] in, e.g., *dempster, empty, Hampton*, is commonly silent throughout the whole of the ModE period and is still so today. In foreign words initial *p* is mostly silent before [n, s, t], e.g. in *pneumatic, psalm, psalter, ptisan, Ptolemy*. A few of these words derive from OE or OF forms without *p*; cf. OE *sealm*, 'psalm', OF *sautier, tisane*.

[b]

§168 The articulation of the voiced bilabial plosive [b] has remained unchanged. Examples: *bee* [biː], *rib* [rib].

Loss of final *b* after [m], as in *climb, comb, lamb, womb* [klaim] etc., is attested in the 16th century.[96] In rarer words, like *iamb* etc., [b] is pronounced (spelling pronunciation or Lat. influence).[97] Medial [b] was also lost occasionally in earlier ModE, e.g. in *chamber, humble*, which are nowadays pronounced [tʃeimbə, hʌmbl]; [b] is still silent in *ambsace* and in *plumber* [plʌmə] (after *plumb*).

After final [b] had been lost, a *b* was sometimes added after [m], e.g. in *limb, numb* [lim, nʌm] from ME *lim, nume*. In *debt, doubt, subtle* [det, daut, sʌtl] a *b* was added on etymological grounds (Lat. *debita*[98], *dubitare, subtilis*).

[t]

§169 The articulation of the voiceless alveolar plosive [t] has remained unchanged. Examples: *time* [taim], *hat* [hæt].

---

[96] The loss had occurred by about 1300 in the North (Jordan, §211).

[97] The *b* of *iamb* is in fact often silent; cf. EPD.

[98] I.e., popular Latin **debita* for classical *debitum*, needed to explain OF *det(t)e* (fem.); but Ekwall is rather too precise, for it is the classical form which has caused *b* to be added in the English (and formerly sometimes in the French) spelling.

G

§170 Latin and French [t] in words of Greek origin is often written *th*. This spelling was also introduced into England, and was not uncommonly transferred to non-Greek words like *Thames*, *Thanet* etc. Gradually this *th* began to be pronounced as [θ]. [t] is still used in *Thames* (but [θ] in *Thanet*), *Thomas*, *thyme*, *Anthony*, *phthisic*, sometimes in *phthisis*.[99] The retention of the [t] after [s], partly alongside [θ], as in *asthma*, *Esther*, *isthmus*, *posthumous*,[1] is probably to be ascribed, at least in part, to a dislike for the sound-group [sθ]. In other words [θ] has gradually prevailed. In the 18th century [t] for *th* was commoner than now. Elphinston 1790 has, e.g., [t] in *apothecary*, *Caithness*, *Catherine*, *Dorothy*, *Theobald*,[2] which nowadays have [θ]. Also with [θ] nowadays are *anthem*, *authentic*, *author*, *mathematics*, *Matthew*, *panther*, *theatre* etc.

§171 [tj] in a weakly stressed syllable has often become [tʃ], both in words like *righteous*, *Christian*, *question*, where [j] derives from [i, e], and also in *creature*, *actual* etc., where [t] preceded [juː] from [iu]. [tʃ] is attested in the latter half of the 17th century by grammarians, and by spellings rather earlier. In the 18th century [tʃ] was current in most words of this kind; according to Walker 1791 in, e.g., *bestial*, *celestial*, *piteous*, *plenteous*, *guttural*, *overture* (he has [tj], however, in e.g. *frontier*, *latitude*, *signature*). In the 19th century a reaction against the pronunciation [tʃ] set in. Today, words in *-tial*, *-tier*, *-teous*, and the like (e.g. *bestial*, *courtier*, *frontier*, *beauteous*, *courteous*, *piteous*, *bastion*) are in general more often pronounced with [tj] or [ti] than with [tʃ].[3] Only very common words like *Christian*, *question*, have more often [tʃ]. [tʃ] has fared better where *tu* is written. In everyday words in *-tune*, *-ture*, *-tual*, *-tuous* etc. (such as *fortune*, *adventure*, *feature*, *furniture*, *actual*, *effectual*) [tʃ] is the usual pronunciation, although [tj] is not uncommon, especially before [u]; thus, e.g., [fiːtʃə, əd'ventʃə; æktʃuəl, æktjuəl]. Less familiar words have [tj] more often than [tʃ], e.g. *overture*, *importune*, *latitude*, *multitude*,[4] *statute* etc. The final syllable in these cases usually has a subsidiary stress; thus, e.g., [ouvətjuə, im'pɔːtjun, lætitjuːd]. For

---

[99] EPD most commonly [θ-] in *phthisic*, *phthisis*; also [fθ-] after the spelling.

[1] EPD gives both [-θ-] and [-t-] as rare in *asthma*, usually [æsmə]. The *h*-spelling in *posthumous* is due to a mistaken etymology which connected the word with Latin *humus* 'earth, soil'.

[2] EPD gives [t-] as surviving in old-fashioned speech, though [t-] is usual in the place name *Theobalds* in Hertfordshire.

[3] [tʃ] appears to be obsolete now in these words in RP.

[4] EPD only [juː] in *latitude*, *multitude*.

many words it is difficult to lay down definite rules, e.g. for *literature*, *statue*, *virtue* [litərətʃə, -tjuə; stætju, -tʃu; vəːtju, -tʃu]. In general the pronunciation here varies considerably, but evidently [tj] is gaining ground.[5]

[tj] remains before a stressed vowel, e.g. in *tube*, *tutor* [tjuːb, tjuːtə]. [tʃ] here is vulgar or provincial.[6]

§172 [t] has frequently been lost, especially between consonants, and particularly between [s] and [l, m, n], and before [s]. The influence of the written form, however, or of related words, often operates, so that [t] is pronounced here also. The loss is generally established in *fancy* from *fantasy* (where the *t* is no longer written), and in *ostler*, *bristle*, *castle* etc., *Christmas*, *chestnut*, *fasten*, *listen* etc., *often*, *waistcoat* [weskət], *wristband* [ris-, rizbənd],[7] *mortgage* etc., although [t] is sometimes used, especially in formal speech.[8] In rapid, less careful speech, [t] is more widely dropped, e.g. in cases like *acts*, *perfectly*, *roast beef*, *Saint Paul's* etc. [sənt-, sən'pɔːlz]. In these and similar cases the loss is attested with certainty from the 16th century or earlier. [t] is lost more rarely after a vowel, as in *boatswain* (cf. §134), and in less careful speech in cases like *a great deal*, *sit down*.

[d]

§173 The articulation of the voiced alveolar plosive [d] has remained unchanged. Examples: *day* [dei], *god* [gɔd].

§174 [dj] has often become [dʒ], at the same time as the change of [tj] to [tʃ], both in words like *soldier*, *tedious*, and in words like *educate*, *verdure*. In the 18th century [dʒ] was extremely common in words of this kind. Walker 1791 has it not only in cases like *soldier*, *grandeur*, *verdure*, but also in *assiduous*, *educate*, *odious*, *procedure*, and others. Today, [dʒ] is much less common. It is still used in a few words, as in *soldier*, *grandeur*, *verdure* [souldʒə, grændʒə, vəːdʒə].[9] In most others, like *cordial*, *hideous*, *India(n)*, *odious*, *radium*, *educate*, *individual*, *residue* etc., [dj] is certainly much commoner than [dʒ].

[5] It is not clear that this is still so. Much depends on the individual word.

[6] Though not mentioned by EPD, [tʃ] may certainly be heard here today in speech which is neither vulgar nor provincial.

[7] Now usually [weiskout, ris(t)bænd] under the influence of the spelling. See §§21 note 30, 153 note 72.

[8] Not in all; commonly in *often*, *waistcoat*, *wristband*, sometimes in *Christmas*, *chestnut*.

[9] EPD still gives [dʒ] as more common than [dj] in *soldier*, *grandeur*, *verdure*.

In these also usage varies, but it is clear that [dʒ] is always less common.[10]

Before a stressed vowel [dj] remains, as in *due, duke* [djuː, djuːk]. [dʒ] here is vulgar or provincial.[11]

§175   Loss of [d].

[d] has frequently been lost medially between [n] and a consonant; e.g. in *grandfather, -mother* etc., *handkerchief, handsome* etc., *and* (as in *bread and butter* etc.), *Windsor*; cf. also *grannam* from *grandam*.[12] In rapid speech [d] is more widely dropped, as in *landlady, landscape, grindstone, windlass, almonds*[13] etc. Loss in these or similar cases is attested throughout the whole of the ModE period. [d] has been restored in, e.g., *London* (according to Elphinston 1765 *Lunnon* or *Lunnun*), *Wednesday*, nowadays [wednzdi] as well as [wenzdi]; spellings like *Wensdai* are found in the 14th century.

[d] has often been lost in final position after a long vowel + [n], as in *groin* 'loins' (ME *grinde*), *lawn* 'grass-plot' (Fr. *lande*), *woodbine* (OE *-binde*). But [d] is pronounced in PresE where *d* is retained in the spelling, as in *bind, bound*. The loss occurred in the EModE period. In *almond, diamond, d* was often silent in earlier ModE.

§176   Since final *d* after *n* was often silent in EModE, *d* was often added without etymological justification. In several cases the spelling has influenced the pronunciation. Examples: *bound* 'ready to start' (ON *būenn*), *hind* 'servant' (ME *hīne*), *pound* 'to crush' (OE *pūnian*), *round* 'to whisper' (OE *rūnian*), *sound* 'noise' (Fr. *son*), all pronounced with [d].[14] *Ribband* beside *ribbon* (Fr. *ruban*) may have been influenced by *band*.

[k]

§177   Two [k] sounds are attested in ModE. According to Wallis 1653 *c* before front vowels was pronounced *cy*, e.g. in *can* (*cyan*), but not before other vowels as in *call, come*. In the 18th and 19th centuries the addition of [j] after *c, k,* is often mentioned by orthoepists, e.g. by Walker 1791 in *card, cart, kind* etc. It has been rightly concluded from observations of this kind that in earlier ModE a

---

[10] EPD gives [dʒ] variants only for *educate, individual*.

[11] Cf. §171 note 6.

[12] *grannam* is now obsolete.

[13] EPD gives pronunciations without [d] as most usual in *landlady, landscape,* and as equally common with [-nd-] in *grindstone*.

[14] For a different view of the origin of [-d] in these words, see Dobson, §§434–6.

palatal [k] was frequently pronounced before front vowels, which could easily give the impression of being [kj]. The palatal [k] was frequently preserved even after the change of certain front vowels to velar or central vowels (thus in words like *card, kind, skirt*). The antiquity and diffusion of this palatal [k] are not known.[15] Today it is rare,[16] and usually what is essentially the same velar [k] is pronounced before all vowels. Examples: *cat* [kæt], *king* [kiŋ], *take* [teik].

§178   Initial [k] before [n] was lost in the 17th century, as in *knife* [naif], *know* [nou], but *acknowledge* [ək'nɔlidʒ]. In the 17th century several intermediate stages are attested, such as [tn] (cf. the common older pronunciation *Twit'nam* for *Twickenham*), hn (probably voiceless [n]; e.g. in Cooper 1685).

Medially [k] was lost in EModE in words like *corpuscle, muscle,* in *blackguard* [blægaːd], and in *asked* [aːs(k)t].

The spellings *drachm, indict, schism, victuals* [dræm, in'dait, sizm, vitlz] from OF *drame,*[17] *enditer, scisme, vitailles,* are purely etymological. In *schedule, verdict* [ʃedjul, skedjul;[18] vəːdikt], the written form has influenced the pronunciation. *Schedule* (EModE, ME *cedule* from French) was pronounced by Walker 1791 with [s]. *Verdict* was often written *verdit* (< OF *verdit*) in EModE. Elphinston 1790 gives silent *c*.

The alternation between [tʃ] and [k] in *seek : beseech, speak : speech,* EModE *reck : retch* 'to care', *ache* [k] (vb) (often written *ake*) : *ache* [tʃ] (sb.) (OE *acan : ece, æce*), originates in the OE period. The sb. *ache* had [tʃ] still *c.* 1700;[19] the spelling *ache* comes from this. *Arch-* [aːtʃ] in *-bishop, -enemy* etc., comes from OE *ærce-,* OF *arche-,* with [tʃ]; *archangel* [aːk] from OF *arc(h)angel* (with [k] retained before *a*).

[g]

§179   In earlier ModE there was a palatal and a velar [g]-sound. The palatal [g] is attested in the same situations and by the same observers as the palatal [k]. Thus Wallis 1653 has it in, e.g., *get, begin* (to be pronounced as *gyet, begyin*), in contrast with velar [g] in *go, gun, goose;* Walker 1791 in *guard, guide* etc. In PresE the

---

[15] It was known to Robinson early in the 17th century and may well be a good deal older (see Dobson, §379 and n.).

[16] It is apparently obsolete now. Cf. Gimson: 'if /iː/ has a very front and tense articulation, the /k, g/ closures will in turn be *near* palatal' (p. 161) (my italics).

[17] ODEE: OF *dragme* or LLat. *dragma.*

[18] [sk-] is now the American pronunciation; it is not in British use. See the note on the pronunciation in OED.

[19] 'Prevalent until *c.* 1820' (ODEE).

palatal [g] is rare,[20] except perhaps in *girl*. Today essentially the same velar [g] is used before all vowels. Examples: *go* [gou], *give* [giv], *rag* [ræg].

§180 Initial [g] was lost before [n] in the 17th century, as in *gnat* [næt], *gnomon* [noumɔn]. The loss is attested by Cooper 1685.[21]

§181 [g] is often lost after [ŋ], and regularly—probably already in ME[22]—when final and preceding a consonant in the same syllable, as in *long, sing, amongst* [lɔŋ, siŋ, ə'mʌŋst]. *Length, strength*, however, are pronounced with [-eŋkθ] as well as [-eŋθ]; [kθ] is already attested in ME. [g] remained before a vowel or a syllabic consonant, e.g. in *anger, finger, angle, single* [æŋgə, æŋgl] etc. Accordingly [ŋg] is regular in comparatives and superlatives like *longer, longest, stronger, younger* etc. [lɔŋgə, lɔŋgist] etc. In most inflected forms and derivatives, however, like *longing, singing* etc., *longish, youngish* etc., and also comparatives and superlatives formed from participles like *cunning* etc., [ŋ] is used today, evidently under the influence of the positives (*long, cunning* etc.). Gil 1619 still has regular [ŋg] in forms like *belongeth, hanging, springing*. [g] is also usually preserved before a voiced consonant in words like *angry, hungry, anguish, language, sanguine*, but not in the derivatives of words in [ŋ], such as *strongly*. *England, English*, vary. In names like *Birmingham, Sempringham*, Gil 1619 has [ŋg], while today [ŋ] is used. Probably [g] regularly remained if the [h] was silent, but dropped if the [h] was pronounced or intended.

§182 *Phlegm* [flem] goes back to OF *fleume*. In *expugn, sign*, [iks'pjuːn, sain] etc., *gn* is a traditional spelling for [n] from OF *n* mouillé. It is not clear whether, in words like *diaphragm, paradigm* [-fræm; -daim, -dim[23]], the loss of g has taken place on English soil or not.[24]

Medially, *gm, gn*, are mostly pronounced [gm, gn], e.g. in *phleg-matic, assignation, cognition, cygnet, impregnable, signal, signet*. To a certain extent we have here undoubtedly the influence of the spelling. This influence is unquestionable in cases like (*re*)*cognizance, recognize*,

[20] Apparently obsolete now (see §177, note 16).

[21] And by earlier 17th century sources. There was also a development of initial *gn-* to [kn]. See Dobson, §418.

[22] Only in Eastern dialects. In educated London English the loss occurred about 1600. See Dobson, §§399, 412.

[23] [-dim] appears to be obsolete.

[24] It probably did, by analogy with *-gn* in words like *expugn, sign*. In French *diaphragme, paradigme* the g is pronounced [g].

physiognomy, where *g* was silent in EModE, but is today for the most part pronounced.[25] Regularly developed are certainly *assignee* [æsi'niː], *poignant* [poinənt],[26] *seignior* [siːnjə].[27] But [gm, gn] are probably to be ascribed partly to Latin influence; it is to be noted also that in French [g] is pronounced in a few cases of this kind, such as *cognat*, *inexpugnable*, and (sometimes) in *signet*.

---

[25] EPD gives *recognize* with [g] only, *physiognomy* with [n] only.
[26] But also [-nj-, -gn-] now.
[27] Now usually [seinjə], rarely [siːn-].

MORPHOLOGY

I. THE SUBSTANTIVE

CASE

§183 In the late ME period only scanty remains were left of the rich system of OE case-inflexions. Except for the basic form there was only a genitive. In the singular this usually had the ending *-es*, which had originally belonged only to certain masculine and neuter substantives. Substantives which had the ending *-es* in the plural added no further ending in the genitive plural; as a rule the ending here was also *-es*.

The ending *-es* became [ez] in ME. Later the [e] was syncopated except after sibilants, whence [z] became [s] after voiceless consonants.

This type of genitive formation is the one still current today. However, in the course of the ModE period the spelling has been regulated so that the genitive ending is written *'s* and the genitive plural without ending is indicated by an apostrophe. Examples: *king's* [kiŋz], *cat's* [kæts], *prince's* [prinsiz]; pl. *kings'*, *men's* [menz], etc.

The *of*-genitive developed in ME.

§184 A genitive without ending, which derives, however, only partly from OE forms, existed in late ME, especially in words ending in *-s*, in proper names, and in other personal names. In EModE, words ending in *-s* were still often unchanged in the genitive singular, especially disyllables and polysyllables, more rarely in the case of monosyllables (e.g. *his mistres beautie* (Sidney), *Pythagoras time, his horse back* (Shakespeare), etc.). Since the 17th century the genitive in such words has been indicated by an apostrophe or *'s*. Both spellings still occur; *'s* is probably the commoner. The pronunciation in both cases is usually [iz]. However, the genitive without ending is kept in expressions like *for conscience sake*.

§185 In ME, and still in the 16th and 17th centuries (more rarely later), the genitive of masculine sbs. ending in *-s* was frequently formed by placing *his* after it, as in *Mars his heart* (Shakespeare), *Aeneas his voyage* (Addison). Less commonly we find *his* after other sbs., or *her, their*. Examples: *Pan his pype* (Lyly), *for Jesus Christ his sake* (Prayer Book 1662), *the Queen her private practice* (Fuller 1655).

§186 Regularly developed genitive forms like *calves, wives* (cf. *calves, wives* (pl.)) are not uncommon in EModE. Examples: *The old Wiues Tale* (title of a play by Peele), *his wiues name* (Bible 1611), even *a beeues fat* (Ben Jonson). Today such forms only occur in compounds like *calvesfoot*.

PLURAL

1. Regular plural formation

§187 In most ME dialects and in the standard language the ending *-es* (< OE *-as*) was extended to most sbs. This ending developed phonetically exactly like the genitive ending *-es*, and thus appears today as [z, s, iz]. Examples: *dogs* [dɔgz], *cats* [kæts], *fishes* [fiʃiz].

2. Irregular plural formation

§188 Certain OE sbs. had by regular sound-change [f, s, θ] finally and [v, z, ð] medially. This alternation has often survived to the present day, in that the singular has [f, s, θ] and the plural [v, z, ð]. The alternation of [s:z] has remained only in *house*: [haus, hauziz]. The alternation of [f:v] occurs in numerous words, such as *knife, leaf, life, loaf, calf, half, shelf, wolf* etc. (pl. *knives* etc.). In a few cases the alternation has been set aside, sometimes in favour of [f], as in *cliff, roof, turf* (pl. *cliffs* etc.), sometimes in favour of [v], as in *glove, grave* (OE *glōf, græf*). There is variation in the case of *hoof, wharf* (pl. *-fs, -ves*). A few still had the alternation in EModE; hence plurals like *cleeves* (from *cliff*), *turves* occur.[1] Foreign words have sometimes adopted the alternation by analogy. Thus *beef, scarf* have mostly the plural *beeves, scarves*; in EModE the plural *grieves* (from *grief*) occurs. The alternation of [θ] and [ð] has been retained in several words containing a long vowel in PresE, namely in *bath, path, oath, mouth, sheath, wreath* [ba:θ, ba:ðz], etc.[2] The plurals

---

[1] *turves* still survives.
[2] *oaths, sheaths, wreaths* now have [θs] also.

[baːðz, paːðz] are new formations; historically [beiðz, peiðz] would have been expected (ME *bāþes* etc.). The alternation developed later in *lath* [laːθ, laːðz],[3] from OE *læþþ*-[4] with [θ] throughout, and probably in *truth, youth*. *Clothes* [klouðz] 'garments', is the old plural of *cloth* [klɔθ] 'fabric', earlier also 'garment'; the plural of *cloth* is now [klɔθs, klɔːðz].[5] A few words have generalized the [θ], such as *heath* [hiːθ], *breath, hearth* etc. *Earth* [əːθ], plural [əːθs],[6] originally had [ð] throughout; OE form *eorðe* (cf. §142).

§189 In a few cases the ending [s] occurs after a voiced sound. *Dice* from *die* 'cube' goes back to OF *dez. Pence* (cf. *penny*) has been borrowed from compounds like *sixpence*, ME *sixpens*; in this case the *e* of the ending was lost before the change of [s] > [z]. The older plurals *bellows, gallows*, still [beləs, gæləs] in Walker 1791, derive from ME *belous, galous* etc., with subsidiary stress on the second syllable. The change of [s] > [z] only took place after an unstressed vowel.

§190 The ME ending -(*e*)*n* (OE -*an* of the *n*-stems) was retained in certain words in earlier ModE, as in *ashen, eyen, hosen, oxen, peasen* (OE *ascan* etc.). Of these only *oxen* is in living use today. -*n* was sometimes added analogically in ME, as in *schon* 'shoes', *housen, children*, and, with *i*-mutation, *breþ(e)ren* (OE *brōðor, brōðru*), *kīn* (OE *cȳ*) 'cows', which are also preserved in EModE (*children, brethren* still today). *Brethren* was still in use in its literal sense in the 16th century, but was soon for the most part displaced by the new formation *brothers*, which was also frequent in the 16th century. *Kine* was the usual form in the 16th century (also in the Bible 1611); *cows* is first recorded in the OED from 1607.

§191 Of the OE mutation plurals *feet, geese, lice, men* (*women*), *mice, teeth*, are left. The alternation of [u] and [i] in the first syllable of *woman* [wumən : wimin] developed in ME.

§192 The plural often has the same form as the singular.

(a) A few such plurals are survivals of OE forms. Strong neuters were frequently unchanged in the nom. and acc. pl. in OE, like

---

[3] EPD gives the [θs] plural as more common now.

[4] This is a presumed etymology; OE *læþþ*- is not in fact recorded.

[5] EPD notes (i) that plural [ɔː] forms are only used by those who use [ɔː] in the singular; (ii) that a variant [klɔːθs] is frequent in the sense 'kinds of cloth' but not for 'pieces of cloth'.

[6] EPD records, as a less common variant, [əːðz]. This is the plural which is historically to be expected, but it is not certain that it has had a continuous existence; Cooper 1685 explicitly denies that *earths* has [ð].

dēor, hors, pl. *dēor, hors*. A few words kept this type of formation
in ME, and the PresE plurals *deer, sheep, swine* are vestiges of it.
In EModE plurals like *pound, weapon, year* (<OE *pūnd, wǣpen,
gēar*) were still current. The plural *hose* comes from OE *hosan*,
similarly *pease* from OE *piosan* (sing. EModE *pease* < OE **piosu*[7]);
later, however, the sing. *pease* was displaced by the new formation
pea.

(b) Words ending in *-s* were often unchanged in the plural in ME
and EModE. They are for the most part Fr. words in *-s* which were
unchanged in the plural in Fr., as in *case, sense, verse* (Fr. *cas*, pl. the
same); but other words followed suit, e.g. Fr. words in *-ess* (such as
duchess, Fr. *duchesse*, pl. *-s*), and native words like *witness*. Shakespeare has, e.g., such plurals as *corpse, sense, mightiness, balance*.

(c) *Fish, fowl*, and the names of animals are often without ending
in ME and ModE. *Fish, fowl*, had the ending *-as* in OE, but are
already frequently unchanged in the plural in ME. Also, several
names of fish, such as *haddock, ling, mackerel, salmon*, and a few
names of birds, like *mallard, partridge, teal*, are found unchanged
in the plural in ME. In the course of the ModE period this plural in
both categories has gained ground considerably. Today, most fish-
names can form their plural without an ending, and a few have
solely or predominantly this form, such as *carp, mackerel, pike,
salmon, trout*, while others have only, or mostly, the *-s* plural, like
eel, herring,[8] *shark*. A few names of game-birds like *curlew, duck,
grouse, ptarmigan, teal, widgeon* are frequently unchanged in the
plural, while others, like *partridge, pheasant*, have almost exclusively
the *-s* plural. In the course of the ModE period the plural without
ending has been extended also to the names of those quadrupeds
which are hunted for their flesh or hide. Isolated examples are to
be found in the 17th and 18th centuries; in wider use, however, the
plural without ending in this category is later. Most of the words in
question are names of non-European animals like *antelope, bison,
buffalo, caribou, eland, giraffe, moose, springbuck* etc., but also
words like *boar, roe(buck)*, are found with uninflected plural. Also
names of beasts of prey are sometimes uninflected, like *puma, tiger*.

[7] Ekwall '(zu fne. *pease*, ae. *piosu*)'. Ekwall's *piosu*, though not starred in the
German text, is presumably intended as a hypothetical form (cf. *peru* beside *pere*
'pear') to account for the back-mutation which gives *io*, later *eo* (whence ulti-
mately ME *ę̄* attested by the ModE spelling with *ea*). But the recorded *piose*
beside *pise* is sufficiently explained from the inflected forms.
[8] But commonly *a shoal of herring* etc.

The uninflected plural is in general current use particularly in the language of sport, but is by no means confined to it.

This plural is to be explained chiefly by the use of numerous words of this kind as names of commodities. From *fish* 'fish as food', e.g., a collective *fish* was easily developed (cf. *cattle* etc.), and hence a plural *fish*. Later this plural gained ground by analogy; as regards the names of quadrupeds the words *deer*, *sheep*, *swine* have been to some extent responsible.

(d) In ME and EModE words like *board*, *brick*, *lath*, *nail*, *tile*, were often uninflected in the plural; cf. *let vs make bricke and burne them* in the Bible 1611. The plurals *cask*, *pearl* were still in use in the 18th century; *sail* has the plural *sail* 'ships' today. A few of these plurals, too, are to be explained by the use of the words as names of materials (e.g. *board*, *brick*, *pearl*); the remainder are probably analogical new formations. *Craft* 'ships' (in use since the 17th century) is elliptical for *vessels of small craft* (OED).[9]

(e) Names of weapons and projectiles, like *ball*, *cannon*, *cartridge*, *shot*,[10] are often unchanged in the plural. *Shot* often means 'shooting weapons collectively' in ME, and goes back to OE *gescot* 'a shooting weapon; such weapons collectively'.[11] From the collective *shot* there developed the plural *shot*, and on the model of this the plurals *ball*, *cannon* etc., found from the 16th century onwards, are new formations.

(f) Measure-, weight-, time-, and price- words were largely uninflected in ME in the plural. A few of these uninflected plurals derive from uninflected plurals in OE, such as *pound*, *year*, *month* (< OE *pūnd*, *gēar*, *mōnað*), or OE plurals in *-u*, *-an*, *-e* (> ME *-e*), like *winter*, *yoke*, *mile* (< OE *wintru*, *geocu*, *mīle*), or OE genitives, which occurred in cases like *sex fingra brād* (*fingra* > ME *fingre*, *finger*); others are analogical new formations. In earlier ModE such plurals were commoner than now. Shakespeare has, e.g., *foot*, *pound*,

---

[9] OED in fact says 'probably elliptical'.

[10] *shot* never has *-s* when the sense is 'lead shot'. *Ball* is obsolete as a term for a projectile.

[11] Ekwall uses the German word *Geschütz*, which now means 'gun, cannon', but from the context he seems to be using it as a collective to describe shooting weapons in general. Even so there is some inaccuracy. OE *gesc(e)ot* means 'the collection of weapons necessary for shooting' and also 'missile'; but in ME, though *shot* is used to mean 'a missile' and 'missiles collectively', it is apparently not used as 'weapons for shooting', individually or collectively, of which OED's earliest instances date from the late 16th century. Perhaps Ekwall intended *Geschoss* 'missile' where in fact *Geschütz* is printed.

shilling, year. Elphinston 1765 gives a long list of plurals of this sort, such as *stand (of arms)*, *bushel (of coals)*, *coil (of ropes)*, *load, ton*. Many are still in use, like *brace, dozen, head, hundred-weight, pair, score, stone*.

II. THE ADJECTIVE

§193   The adjective in ModE has no other inflexions than comparative and superlative.

The OE ending of the comparative, *-ra*, became ME *-re, -ere, -er*, ModE *-er*; the superlative endings *-est(a)*, *-ost(a)* > ME *-est(e)*, ModE *-est* [ist]. In the ME period comparatives and superlatives with *more, most*, developed. These types of comparison were, to begin with, used more or less without distinction. Already in EModE, however, there is an unmistakable tendency to restrict comparison with *-er, -est* to shorter adjectives, and that with *more, most* to longer ones. The rules operating today have only gradually evolved from there.

§194   Irregular comparison.

Of the OE mutated comparative and superlative forms only *elder, eldest* are in use today. In the 16th century *lenger, lengest, strenger, strengest* (from *long, strong*) are recorded.

Comparatives and superlatives with shortening of the stem vowel (like *gretter* from *great*) were still quite common in the 16th century. Of these only *latter*,[12] *utter* remain today, and they are no longer true comparatives.

Of the other irregular forms, the following are still in use: *better, best* from *good*; *worse, worst* from *bad* etc.; *less, least* from *little*; *more, most* from *much, many*; *further, furthest* and *farther, farthest* from *far*; *next* means mostly 'next-in-order' and is rarely a superlative of *near*. In earlier ModE others also were in use. Thus Shakespeare has the comparative *far* (< OE *feorra*). *Near* (< OE *nēar*, comparative of *nēah* (adv.) > *nigh*) was still current as a comparative in the 17th century. *Mo* (originally an adv. = G. *mehr*) was often in EModE the comparative of *many*.[13]

---

[12] But *latter* derives from OE *lætra*, and is therefore not an example of shortening.

[13] Already in OE *mā* was used as an indeclinable neuter noun, in effect the comparative of the indeclinable *fela* 'much, many'. The use as a comparative adjective develops from this in later OE and ME; it is usually, as Ekwall says, the comparative of *many*, but sometimes of *much*.

Double comparatives and superlatives were frequent in EModE. Shakespeare often has constructions like *more better, most unkindest*; by the 18th century these were no longer allowable. On the other hand, *lesser* (instead of *less*) is still in attributive use, and the corresponding form *worser* is hardly to be considered entirely dead.[14]

The suffixes *-more, -most* were employed in ME mostly to form the superlative (rarely the comparative) of adverbs (like *inmost* from *in*), or the superlative of the comparative of adverbs (like *innermost* from *inner*). This form of comparison is in living use in ModE and has even gained ground. Thus superlatives like *lattermost, nearmost, nextmost*, even *bettermost, highmost* are to be found. Of recent origin are superlatives of nouns used as adjectives, like *centremost, sternmost, topmost*.

III. Numerals

§195 The ordinal numbers, with the exception of *first, second, third*, are formed from the cardinal numbers by means of the ending *-(e)th*. In EModE and up to the 18th century, however, the forms *fifth, sixth, twelfth* were frequently pronounced with [t] instead of [θ]; spellings like *fift* are rare after the 16th century. *Fift, sixt, twelft* are the old forms (OE *fifta* etc.). The form *eight* existed for a long time (according to the OED, up to the 19th century) alongside *eighth* (OE *eahtoða*).

IV. The Article

§196 The definite article was already indeclinable in ME and had acquired the form *the*. Before a vowel, and in enclitic position, the vowel was often lost in ME and EModE: so, e.g., in Shakespeare *th'other, i'th'name* etc. This shortened form was later abandoned and the PresE distinction evolved, whereby the article when emphatic is pronounced [ðiː], otherwise [ði] before a vowel and [ðə] before a consonant. This distinction is mentioned by Walker 1791.

---

[14] Though virtually only in phrases like *the worser part*.

§197   The indefinite article (originally identical with the numeral *one*) had the forms *a*, *an* in the late ME period, but distribution according to the initial sound of the following word had not yet been fully established. In EModE, as today, *a* was used before a consonant, *an* before a vowel, but also frequently before [h] (as in *an hand*, *an hundred*). Words like *ewe*, *union*, had an initial vocalic sound in EModE, and so *an* was used before them according to the rule. *An* is still occasionally written as a traditional spelling before such words. The indefinite article is now [ei, æn] when emphatic, [ə, ən] when weakly stressed.

V. THE PRONOUNS

PERSONAL PRONOUNS

§198   In late ME, of the OE inflected forms, only a subject-form corresponding to the OE nominative, and an object-form corresponding to the OE dative (*I*, *me*; *he*, *him*, etc., < *ic*, dat. *mē*; *hē*, dat. *him*) were still in use. In ModE these pronouns have for the most part undergone only phonetic changes. They are often unemphatic and therefore prone to marked alteration; sometimes an emphatic and an unemphatic form can be distinguished.[15] From the unemphatic forms there derive ModE *I* (< ME *ich*, OE *ic*; cf. the ending -*ly* from OE -*līc*), *us* (< OE *ūs*), *you* [juː] from EModE, ME [ju][16] (ME *you* [juː] became EModE [jou] with the diphthong in *now*), *it* (< OE *hit*), *them* (cf. ME, EModE *theym*). In EModE there was a weakly stressed form of *thou* [ðu]. The weakly stressed form often lost its vowel in EModE; cf., e.g., *th'art* (= *thou art*), *h'is* (= *he is*), *sh'ad* (= *she had*), *'tis*, *in't* (= *it is*, *in it*) in Shakespeare and others.

In EModE, instead of *he*, *a* (< ME *a*, *ha* of uncertain origin) was in use, especially after the verb, as in *quotha* = *quoth he*.

§199   Case-shifts are common in the pronominal field; cf. especially Jespersen, *Progress in Language*, pp. 182 ff. *You* (originally the object-form, OE *ēow*) has also become established as the subject-form.

---

[15] For detailed evidence and discussion, see Dobson, §4.

[16] PresE [juː] does not derive solely from earlier weak-stressed [ju], but also from [jiu], a special development of the ME stressed form [juː]; see Dobson, §178.

In EModE, *ye* was still often used as the subject-form. *You* appears as a subject-form already in the 15th century.

§200 The PresE forms of the personal pronouns are: *I, me, we, us* [ai; miː, mi; wiː, wi; ʌs, əs, s]; *thou, thee; you* [ðau; ðiː, ði; juː, ju, jə][17]; *he, him,* [hiː, (h)i; him, (h)im]; *she, her* [ʃiː, ʃi; həː(r), (h)ə(r)]; *it* [it, t]; *they, them* [ðei;[18] ðem, ðəm]. Beside *them, 'em* [əm] still occurs in colloquial speech, from OE *he(o)m* (*they, them* < ON *þei(r), þeim*).

POSSESSIVE PRONOUNS

§201 The possessive pronouns had become indeclinable in late ME, though *mine, thine* were often used instead of *my, thy* before a vowel. In EModE also we often find *mine, thine* in cases like *mine eyes, mine ears, mine host,* even *mine heart* (e.g. in the Bible 1611). Unemphatic forms of the possessive pronouns also occur. Thus *my* was usually pronounced [mi] in earlier ModE when unemphatic (so still in Walker 1791); today [mi] is rarer than [mai] except in *mylord, -lady*[19] [mi'lɔːd, -'leidi]. *Mine* also had an unemphatic form [min], which is still mentioned by Walker 1806, and even today is heard on the stage.[20] PresE *your* [juə, joə, jɔːə][21] derives perhaps from an unemphatic form, or may have been influenced by *you*; ME *youre* should have given [jauə] (cf. *our*).

§202 The pronoun *its* appeared in the 16th century, and has so far been first found shortly before 1600. In the 16th century *his* was still used with the meaning *its*; the equivalents *of it, thereof,* and even *it* also occurred (the last-named, e.g., in the Shakespeare Folio 1623). The Bible 1611 has only *his, of it, thereof, it*. Beside *their* (< ON *þeira*) *her* (< OE *heora*) is occasionally found in the 16th century.

§203 The PresE forms are: *my* [mai, mi], *our* [auə(r)],[22] *thy* [ðai], *your* [juə, joə, jɔːə;[23] ju, jə]; *his* [hiz, iz], *her* [həː(r), (h)ə(r)], *its* [its],

---

[17] EPD notes that [ju] occurs as a strong (i.e. emphatic) form in *you're* [juə] in PresE.

[18] [ðe] is 'not infrequent' as a weak form, especially before vowels (EPD); [ðe] also occurs as an emphatic form in the single expression *they're* [ðeə].

[19] Both are in very limited use today.

[20] EPD 'in serious drama' when attributive and unemphatic. EPD notes this tradition as also applying to *my*; i.e. [mi] when unemphatic etc. But these pronunciations are rare nowadays.

[21] EPD gives [jɔː] as the main form, does not record [jɔːə].

[22] Also now [aː(r)].

[23] See note 21 above.

their [ðɛə(r), ðə(r)]. Absolute forms: *mine, ours*; *thine, yours*; *his, hers, theirs* [main, auəz,[24] ðain, juəz (etc.), hiz, həːz, ðɛəz].

DEMONSTRATIVE PRONOUNS

§204 Only *that, this* inflect in ModE.

That (OE *þæt*, the form of the nom. and acc. sing. neuter of the pronoun *se*=G. *der*) took over in ME the function of all the OE forms of the sing.; *tho* (OE *þā*, nom., acc. pl.) the function of the OE plural forms. Already in ME *those* (OE *þās*, nom., acc. pl. of *þes* 'this')[25] was associated with *that, tho*, and took the meaning which it now has. In EModE *tho* was soon displaced by *those*, and *that* [ðæt] has now the plural form *those* [ðouz].

§205 *This* derives from OE *þis* (nom., acc. sing. neuter of the pronoun *þes* 'this'), which supplanted the remaining sing. forms in ME. On this form a plural *thise* or *these* was modelled in ME. *Thise* was formed by the addition of the plural-ending *-e* of adjectives to *this*; *these* is of uncertain origin.[26] *Thise* gave EModE *thise, this*, possibly surviving in part in cases like *this ten days*;[27] *these* became ModE *these*, EModE [ðeːz], PresE [ðiːz].

RELATIVE AND INTERROGATIVE PRONOUNS

§206 Only *who* [huː] inflects, gen. *whose* [huːz], dat., acc. *whom* [huːm]. These forms have been current since the late ME period. The OE forms were *hwā*, gen. *hwæs*, dat. *hwām*; *hwæs* was re-formed in ME after the nom. as *whoos*.

INDEFINITE PRONOUNS

§207 Here there is need only to mention that in the 16th and 17th centuries *other*, when used as a sb., often had the form *other*

---

[24] Also now [aːz].

[25] There are difficulties with this explanation; see, e.g., Mustanoja, *Middle English Syntax*, Part I, pp. 169–70.

[26] In part ME *þese* is from EME *þise* with lengthening of *i* to *ē* in the open syllable; hence EModE [ðiːz]. In part it is from ME *þes* with addition of *-e*, giving later ME *þēse*; hence EModE *these* [ðɛːz], later [ðeːz] (the more usual form).

[27] *ten days* is probably treated as a unit of time here (cf. *fortnight*) and is therefore preceded by the sing. *this*. EModE *this* used as a true plural may in part be from ME *þise* as Ekwall says; but it is mainly a survival of the ME use of *þis* as an uninflected plural.

H

in the plural.[28] The earlier ModE form (*the*) *t'other* instead of *the other* derives from ME *that other*.

The remaining pronouns give no cause for comment.

VI. THE VERB

§208   The changes in verbal inflexion in the course of the ModE period are not very considerable. Already towards the end of the ME period verbal inflexion had become markedly simplified through phonetic and analogical influences. Through the loss of final unstressed vowels forms that were different in OE had frequently fallen together. E.g., through analogy the *i* in the present stem of numerous verbs was set aside (OE *lōcian* > ME *loken*).

At the beginning of the ModE period the composite verb-forms were developed, such as the perfect and pluperfect, the progressive form (*I am reading*, in EModE also *a-reading*), and the periphrasis with *to do*. The rules for the use of these forms, however, were frequently different in EModE from what they are today.

A. The Preterite and Past Participle†

1. STRONG VERBS‡

§209   The most important change in the strong verbs in ME was the loss of the pret. pl. as a separate form. Towards the end of the

---

[28] This uninflected plural represents the original adjectival inflection (OE *ōþre*, plural), and it survived in fact into the 18th century. The plural *others*, modelled on the plural of nouns, is first found in the 16th century.

† (Ekwall's note). We shall deal first with the formation of the pret. and part., then with the personal endings and related matters. A separate section is devoted to the forms of a few verbs showing marked divergences, especially auxiliary verbs.

‡ (Ekwall's note). The traditional division of verbs into strong and weak may be kept in ME and ModE on the whole without difficulty. Only a few verbs whose stems end in -*d*, -*t* present any problems. PresE *slide slid slid* goes back to OE *slīdan slād slidon sliden*, *chide chid chid* to OE *cīdan cīdde cīdd*. It is really a matter of taste whether *slide*, *chide* should be considered as strong or weak verbs. These difficulties can be disregarded here.

Also, the division of strong verbs into six gradation classes and a reduplicating class can be retained. In the course of the ModE period the classes certainly become much confused.

15th century the pret. pl. had usually the same form as the sing.;
in the 16th century only isolated remains of a separate pl. form are
to be found. Accordingly, while in OE and ME four terms (pres.,
pret. sing., pret. pl., past part.) are necessary to display the gradation
changes, in ModE three forms suffice.

The pret. sing. often took over the vowel of the pret. pl., especially
where the participle had the same vowel. Examples: *broke*[29] instead
of *brak*, *bound* instead of *band* after the pret. pl. and part. *broken*,[30]
bounden.

The old alternation between the voiced and unvoiced fricative, as
in OE *rīsan*, ME *rise* [z]: OE *rās*, ME *roos* [s], OE *drīfan*, ME *drive* [v]:
OE *drāf*, ME *droof* [f], had already in ME been usually set aside in
favour of the voiced sound.

§210 In ModE the pret. and past part. have frequently influenced
each other. The part. often influenced the form of the pret., as in
beat with EModE [e:] instead of [i:] after *beaten*, perhaps *writ* instead
of *wrote* after *written*, or even took over the function of the pret., as
in *sung* (pret.) for *sang* after the part. *sung*.[31] Vice-versa, the form of
the pret. often occurs with the function of the part.; cf. *shook* (part.)
instead of *shaken*; *fell*, *held* (part.) instead of *fallen*, *holden*.

§211 The past part. had the ending *-en* in OE, whence ME *-en*, *-e*.
In ME the ending in northern English was mostly *-en* except in verbs
whose stem contained a nasal (as in *come*, *win*, *sink* etc.); the loss
of *-n* is evidently due to phonetic causes. In southern English the
ending was very commonly *-e*; in the midlands there was much
variation.

In EModE, as in northern English, the part. has mostly *-en* except
in the case of verbs with a nasal in the stem. The same rule is valid
on the whole for PresE; accordingly we have *written*, *broken*, *graven*,
fallen, but *come*, *won*, *sunk*, *bound* etc. Forms without *-en*, however,
occur occasionally in all ablaut classes in EModE; participles like

---

[29] Ekwall *brok*, but this has no warrant in OED.
[30] The desire for conciseness has led Ekwall into inaccuracy of statement here;
for though ME *bounden* was both pret. and past part., *broken* was only past part.
Broke began to be used as a pret. only after the distinction of sing. and pl. had
been lost. The ME pret. pl. was *breke(n)* < OE *brǣcon*, *brēcon* (also *brake(n)* from
the ME pret. sing.).
[31] This is not fully accurate. Preterites like *sung*, and probably in part *writ*
instead of *wrote*, derive as much from the ME pret. pl. as from the participle;
for in these verbs the pret. pl. and the participle had the same stem. Cf. §209
above.

fall, stand, shake, e.g., are recorded. These are evidently survivals of
ME forms without *-n.*

In the 17th and 18th centuries *n*-less participles became very
common, much commoner than they are today, even outside class 3,
in classes 1, 2, 4, 5; e.g. *writ, chose, broke, eat* etc., but only *shaken,
fallen, blown.* Only a few of these *n*-less forms, such as *slid, got, eat,*[32]
have survived. Probably participles like *writ, broke,* are mostly to
be interpreted as preterites with participial function, and are thus
analogous to *sat, shook, held* etc.[33]

Class 1

OE type: *rīdan, rād, ridon, riden.*

§212   Most verbs of this class kept their strong inflexion throughout the ME period. New additions in ME were the Scand. *rive,
thrive,* and the Fr. *strive.*[34]

§213   In ModE the pret. has mostly the expected form: *rode,
drove* etc. *Shone* has shortening of the vowel ([ɔ] in Cooper 1685);
smote rhymes with *not* in Shakespeare.

In earlier ModE preterites like *rid, writ,* were current, and are
still to be found in good authors in the 18th century. Especially
common in EModE were *bit, slid; bote, slode* are very seldom
recorded. Forms like *driv,*[35] *ris* belonging to *drive, rise* also occur,
though rather more rarely. Preterites of this kind are extremely
rarely recorded in ME;[36] probably they developed late. For explanation cf. §210. Weak verbs like *chide, hide* (pret. *chid* < OE *cidde* etc.)
may in part have supplied a model; on the other hand the latter
have developed analogical strong participles (*chidden, hidden*).

Preterites like *drave, strave* (e.g. in the Bible 1611) are rare. After

[32] By *eat* Ekwall probably meant the form pronounced [et], no longer used as a
participle in educated speech but still widely current. But see also §243 and note 71.

[33] This is very unlikely; they almost certainly derive from ME participles without
-n, without any break in continuity. It is doubtful whether forms without *-en*
became commoner in the 17th and 18th centuries than they had been in the 16th,
except in individual verbs; there was more variation in the 16th century than
Ekwall seems to allow.

[34] Verbs from French are normally conjugated as regular weak verbs in
English, and weak forms of *strive* were common in ME and survived into ModE.

[35] OED does not record *driv,* and such a form is unlikely since English avoids *v*
in final position. Presumably Ekwall is indicating a pronunciation [driv]. The
phrase 'rather more rarely' is an understatement.

[36] Presumably Ekwall means that they are rare in ME as pret. sing.; pret. pl.
forms with short *i,* variously spelt, were normal.

the 16th century such forms occur chiefly, today exclusively,[37] in poetry. They are to be explained partly as northern English forms (in northern English OE *ā* did not become *ǭ*), partly as analogical formations on the model of *brake* beside *broke* (see §233).

§214   The participle has mostly the regular form in ModE: *driven, risen* etc. The form without *-en* was not much in use in the 16th century. Shakespeare has, e.g., only a few examples of *rid, smit, bestrid*, though often *bit, writ*, beside *bitten* etc. In the 17th and 18th centuries participles of this kind are frequent in good writers. *Slid* still survives; otherwise such forms are rare today.

Participles like *rode, rose* often occur in earlier ModE. Shakespeare has, e.g., *arose, drove, rode, shone, smote, strove, wrote*. They were still current in the 17th and 18th centuries, and *abode, bestrode, shone* are still in use.[38]

§215   The verb *strike* varied in the preterite in EModE between the expected form *stroke*, and *strik, strake, strook, struck*. Of these, *struck* prevailed in the 17th century. The history of the forms *strook, struck*, is disputed. *Strook* [struːk] is perhaps to be explained as a dialectal form of *stroke* [stroːk] (cf. §81); *struck* [struk, strʌk] developed from [struːk]. The participle in EModE had forms like *stricken, stroke, strooke(n), struck(en)*; Shakespeare has *stricken, struck(en), stroke*. Gradually *struck* has displaced the remaining forms except in certain expressions (such as *stricken in years*).

§216   *Bide, glide* have become weak; *abide* varies.[39] *Rive* has pret. *rived*, part. *riven. Shrive, strive, thrive* are sometimes weak in earlier ModE and even today. *Shine* had frequently in earlier ModE pret., part. *shined*.[40]

§217   Present distribution:

[ai – ou – i]: *drive (drove, driven)*; similarly *ride, (a)rise, shrive, smite, strive, thrive, write*.

[ai – i – i]: *bite (bit, bitten), slide (slid, slid)*.

[ai – ou – ou]: *abide, stride (bestride* has pret. *-strode, -strid*, part. *-strid(den), -strode)*.

[ai – ɔ – ɔ]: *shine*.

[ai – ʌ – ʌ]: *strike*.

---

[37] They are now obsolete.

[38] *abode* and *bestrode* are scarcely current as past participles, but *shone* is the regular past participle of *shine*.

[39] *abide* is now exclusively strong, except in *abided by* 'kept to' (the rules).

[40] And still to some extent today.

Class 2

OE type: *crēopan, crēap, crupon, cropen*.

§218   Several verbs of this class became weak in ME: e.g. all
those with *ū* in the present, like *brook, suck* < OE *brūcan, sūcan*; also
flee, lie 'tell a lie', *brew, chew*, and others. A few more had gone out
of use. Those that kept their strong inflexion were greatly altered.
The pret. pl. took over at an early date the *o*-vowel of the part. The
pret. sing. either acquired an *a*-vowel on the model of Class 4, or an
o-vowel through the influence of the pl. and part. OE *cēosan*, ME
chēse, lost its 'grammatical change'.[41]

The verbs in this class were few in number at the beginning of the
ModE period, and furthermore, in the course of the ModE period
several have become weak. The individual verbs show marked variations among themselves.

§219   The pret. usually has an *o*-vowel in ModE (*chose, clove*
etc.), rarely, *a*. The part. has mostly the regular form in *-en* (*chosen,
cloven* etc.) alongside not uncommon *chose, clove* etc., from the
16th to the 18th centuries.

The expected sequence EModE [i:, o:, o:] we find only in *creep,
freeze*. *Creep*, however, has mostly the weak form *crept* in ModE;
crope (pret.), *crope(n)* (part.) were still in use in the 18th century as
literary forms. *Freeze* has lost 'grammatical change'.

§220   The following verbs show special variations:

Seethe (today *-d*) usually had in the 16th and 17th centuries the
pret. *sod*, which is a new formation on the part. in place of *seeth*[42]
(< OE *sēað*), part. *sod(den)*. Today *sodden* is adjectival only.

Fly 'make wing', part. *flown* are derived regularly from OE
flēogan, flogen. *Flew* is a new formation in ME in place of *fleih* etc.
(OE *flēah*) after *threw: thrown* etc.

Choose diverges from the regular type only in the present. The
expected form *chese* is rare after 1500. The usual forms in the ModE
period are *choose* (< OE *cēosan*), and *chuse*, EModE [tʃiuz], whose
origin is disputed.[43] The spelling *chuse* is still to be found *c.* 1800;

---

[41] My inverted commas. By this term Ekwall means the consonantal variation
produced by 'Verner's Law' in the OE conjugation: infinitive *cēosan*, pret. sing.
cēas, but pret. pl. *curon*, past part. *coren*.

[42] *seeth* is a late ME form of the pret. sing.

[43] *choose* develops from *cēosan* by shift of stress to the second element of the
OE diphthong. *Chuse* is best explained as a phonetic variant of *choose* developed
in late ME owing to the influence on the vowel of the preceding palatal consonant.

in pronunciation *choose* and *chuse* were bound to fall together in the 17th century.

Lose (OE *lēosan*, still *leese* in the Bible 1611, e.g.) still had the strong part. *lorn* (*forlorn*, more rarely *-lore*) in the 17th century, and up to *c.* 1600 the pret. *forlore* modelled on it. Today (*for*)*lorn* is adjectival only.[44]

Cleave 'split' (OE *clēofan*) had EModE [eː] in the pres. instead of [iː], probably through the influence of *cleave* 'adhere', and therefore went over to Class 4. In the pret. today, beside *clove*, there is also *clave*,[45] and the weak *cleft, cleaved*; in the part., beside *cloven, clove*, there are also *cleft, cleaved*. *Cleave* 'adhere' has occasionally acquired strong forms from *cleave* 'split'. Beside *cleaved* a pret. *clave*[46] and *clove*, and a part. *clove*[47] still occur.

§221   PresE distribution:

[iː – ou – ou]: *freeze* (*froze, -n*), *cleave* (see above).

[uː – ou – ou]: *choose* (*chose, -n*).

[ai – uː – ou]: *fly* (*flew, flown*).

Class 3

(a) **With stem ending in** **nd, mb.** OE type: *bindan, band, bundon, bunden*. Stem-vowel long.[48]

§222   In late ME the pret. sing. was often influenced by the pl. and part., so that, e.g., *bound* occurs alongside *bond* (*band*). Especially common is *found*, which may in part go back to OE *funde*, by-form of *fand*.

§223   In ModE the forms *bound, found* soon became the sole forms in the pret. In the part. forms like *bounden, founden* still occurred in the 16th century but were soon displaced by *bound* etc.; *bounden*, however, still survives as an adjective (*my b. duty* etc.). All verbs in *-nd* have kept their strong inflexion.

---

[44] This account is inaccurate. (*For*)*lorn* is indeed from the past part. of the OE strong verb (*for*)*lēosan*, but *lose* is from the OE weak verb *losian*, with its vowel affected in pronunciation (but not in the surviving spelling) by the verb *loose*, itself derived from the adjective. The verb *leese* < OE *lēosan* simply became obsolete in the later 17th century, except for its participle *lorn*. (Ekwall obviously wished to explain [uː] in *lose* from ME *ǭ* < OE *ēo* with stress-shift; but stress-shift did not occur in words like *lēosan*—cf. Luick, §265.)

[45] *clave* is no longer current.

[46] See previous note.

[47] The part. *clove* 'adhered' is no longer current.

[48] In later OE; originally short. Often re-shortened in ME, as Ekwall explains below.

Climb is mostly weak throughout the ModE period (pret. and part. *climbed*). In EModE, however, strong forms are not uncommon, for example on the one hand pret. *clomb* (< ME *clǫmb*, OE *clāmb*) and the part. *clomb* formed on it, both still to be found today as archaic forms,[49] on the other hand part. *clum* (< ME *clumben* with shortening of the vowel) on which, after the analogy of *swim, swam, swum*, etc., a new present *clim*, pret. *clam* were modelled.[50]

(b) **With stem ending in *mm, nn, nk, ng*.** Stem-vowel short. OE type: *spinnan, span, spunnon, spunnen*.

§224   Verbs with stems in *-ng* had a long vowel in OE which was shortened in ME, though after the change of *ā* to *ǭ*. In the pret. sing. the vowel was thus properly *o* (*song* etc.). However, the vowel became mostly *a* (*sang* etc.) on the analogy of *drank* etc.; Caxton, e.g., always has *a*. Forms like *sung* occur comparatively rarely in the pret. sing. in ME.

§225   In the 16th century and later the pret. varied between *a*- and *u*- forms, and so one finds not only, as in PresE, forms like *began, drank, sang* etc., and *flung, slunk, spun* etc., but also, e.g., *flang, span, wan, wrang*, and *begun, swum* etc. Shakespeare has e.g. *began, begun; drank, drunk; swam, swum; wan, won;* but only *shrunk, slunk, stunk, swung, wrung*. In the 18th century it looked as though the *a*-forms would be completely displaced. Elphinston 1765 notes that *sang, sank*, and others were on the way to becoming as obsolete as, e.g., *drave* (from *drive*). In the 19th century a reaction set in, and today the *a*-form is in some verbs the only one, as in *begin, swim, drink*, or is at least the usual form, as in *sink, ring, sing*, while most verbs have only, or predominantly, the *u*-form, as in *spin, win, slink, cling, fling, sling, sting, swing, wring*. Variation especially occurs in *shrink, stink*.

§226   The part. sometimes had the ending *-en* still in the 16th century, e.g. *drunken, sunken*; such forms are now poetic only or have adjectival function. Alongside *begun, drunk, sung* etc., forms like *began* etc., were not uncommon in earlier ModE (especially in the 17th to 18th centuries). Shakespeare has *swam. Drank* was still used by good writers (Dickens, Trollope, and others) in the 19th century. Today only *u*-forms are current.

---

[49] *clomb* is now obsolete.

[50] The *clim clam clum* conjugation depends on the loss of final *-b*, which allows the analogy of *swim* (OE *swimman*) to operate; it occurs from ME onwards and is chiefly South-western and Northern.

§227 The verb *run* is only anomalous in the pres. The pret. today is *ran*, the part. *run*; in earlier ModE pret. *run* and part. *ran* also occurred. The pres. had mostly the form *run* already in the 16th century, more rarely *ren* (< ME *renne* < ON *renna*) and *rin* (< ME *rinne* < OE *rinnan* or ON *rinna*). The explanation of the form *run*, already recorded in ME, is uncertain.[51]

§228 The originally weak *dig* has been modelled on *spin, spun, spun* etc. (also *stick, stuck* §237). The part. *dug* is recorded from the 16th century, the pret. *dug* from the 18th.

(c) With stem ending in *l, r* + cons. OE type: *helpan, halp, hulpon, holpen.*

§229 Several of the OE verbs of this class adopted weak inflexions in ME, e.g. *bark, burn, yell, yelp* (OE *beorcan, beornan, gellan, gelpan*). The pret. pl. modelled itself chiefly on the part. (OE *hulpon* > ME *holpen*)[52] and in late ME a pret. sing. with an *o*-vowel (*holp* etc.) was a frequent new formation.[53]

In ModE the verbs belonging here have become weak. In the 16th century the preterites *dolve* of *delve*, *mo(u)lte* of *melt*, for example, the participles *coruen, doluen, molten, throshen, yolden* of *carve, delve, melt, thresh, yield*, were still in use. The strong inflexion of *help* (pret. *holp*, part. *holp, -en*) survived longer; it still exists in archaic and poetic use. *Molten* and *carven* (an odd new formation in place of *corven*) are now used only as adjectives.

(d) OE *feohtan, feaht, fuhton, fohten.*

§230 The pres. *fight* derives regularly from OE *feohtan*. The pret. *faught* (< OE *feaht*) is recorded in the 16th century, but usually this form is replaced by *fought*. *Fought* may be a new formation in ME after the pret. pl. and part. *fought(en)*,[54] or a written form for [fauxt] and due to the influence of *brought* etc. which were often pronounced with [au] (§90). *Foughten* was in use as a participle in the 16th and 17th centuries beside *fought*. The victory of the form *fought* is

---

[51] ODEE regards this as due to levelling through from forms in which *-u-* was original, i.e. in the pret. pl. and past part. Re-formation of the infinitive and present stem on that of the past part. was a fairly common process in ME, because in some strong conjugations (5, 6, 7) the two stems were the same.

[52] But ME spellings with *o* may often conceal a pronunciation with *ŭ*.

[53] This is hardly correct; OED does not record a pret. sing. *holp(e)* until the early 16th century.

[54] The later ME pret. pl. and past part., though spelt the same, must have been pronounced differently, since the former had OE *u*, the latter OE *o*. The *fought* form of the ModE pret. must derive rather from the past part., whose pronunciaiton would develop so as to coincide with that of the older pret. *faught*.

probably to be ascribed in part to the influence of *bring, brought* etc.

§231   PresE distribution:[55]

(a) [ai – au – au]: *bind* (*bound, bound*). Similarly *find, grind, wind*.

(b) [i – æ – ʌ]: *begin* (*began, begun*); cf. §225.

[i – ʌ – ʌ]: *spin* (*spun, spun*); cf. §225.

[ʌ – æ – ʌ]: *run* (*ran, run*).

(d) [ai – ɔː – ɔː]: *fight* (*fought, fought*).

Class 4

OE type: *beran, bær, bǣron, boren.*

§232   To this class were transferred in ME most of the verbs in Class 5 (such as *get, speak, tread, weave*), from Class 6 *heave, swear* (OE *hebban, swerian*), and finally the weak verb *wear* (OE *werian, werede*).

The original short *a* (<OE *æ*) of the pret. sing. was frequently lengthened in ME on the analogy of other forms (thus *bār* beside *bar*, etc.).[56] A new pret. sing. in *o* (*bor* etc.) was often formed in late ME under the influence of the part. *bore(n)* etc. and the pret. pl. *bore(n)* etc. which had been re-formed on the part.[57]

§233   In EModE the pret. varied between *a* and *o*. In the first half of the 16th century the *a*-forms had perhaps the upper hand;[58] in the 17th century, however, they were probably already mostly literary forms. Shakespeare has mostly *o*-forms, and these were *c.* 1700 the prevailing ones in the literary language. *Bare, brake* etc. are subsequently only poetic or archaic.

§234   The part. has mostly -(*e*)*n* (*spoken, sworn* etc.); however, especially in the 17th to 18th centuries, forms like *broke, stole* were common in good writers, and the participles *bespoke, got, hove* are

---

[55] For (c), see §229 above; the verbs are now weak.

[56] This explanation is no longer acceptable. It now seems clear that in ME new pret. plurals (*bare(n)* etc.) were formed on the singulars (*bar* etc.), and that in these disyllabic forms the *a* was lengthened, giving later ME *bāre(n)* etc.; then new singulars with the long vowel were deduced from the plurals, and eventually displaced the old singulars with short *a*. But the latter survived into the 16th century.

[57] The pret. pl. was only sometimes re-formed on the past part.; the normal ME pret. pl. had *e*<OE *ǣ, ē*. But it is true that *o*-forms in late ME are found earlier in the pret. pl. than in the pret. sing.

[58] This is an understatement; *bare, brake, spake* etc., were the normal 16th century forms.

still in use.[59] In verbs like *bear, swear, tear*, the stem-vowel varied for a long time between [ɔ], later [ɔː], and [oː]. A distinction was even made from the 17th century onwards between *borne* [bɔːrn] 'carried' and *born* [bɔːrn] 'born' (e.g. by Cooper 1685). Later, [oː] and [ɔː] regularly fell together before [r]. *Broke* occurs as an adjective ('penniless' etc.).

§235 The vowel of the present has become [iː] in some verbs; in others the change did not take place, and PresE has [ei, ɛə].

Get, tread generally have a short stem-vowel, though a long vowel is still recorded in EModE.

§236 OE *cuman, c(w)ōm, -on, cumen*. Pres. and part. *come* [kʌm] go back to OE *cuman, cumen*. In ME the pret. sing. often had the form *cam*, or, with analogical[60] lengthening, *cām*. The latter (written *came*) is the usual one in ModE; in earlier ModE both *cam* and *come* (< ME *coom*, OE *cōm*) are still found. The part. *comen* is recorded in EModE.

§237 *Stick* goes back to ME *steken* (*stak*, part. *stoken, steken*; OE **stecan*[61] = G. *stechen* 'pierce, fasten' and ME *stiken* (OE *stician*) 'pierce'.[62] These verbs were merged. The present tense *stick* goes back to ME *stiken*. The EModE pret. *stack* (*stake, stoke*) belongs to *steken*. On the pres. *stick* and pret. *stack* the part. *stuck* was formed at an early date on the analogy of *sink, sank, sunk* etc.; later the pret. conformed to the part.

§238 PresE distribution:

[iː – ou – ou]: *steal* (*stole, -en*), similarly *speak, weave*; *heave* (*hove, hove*); *bespeak* (*-spoke*, part. *-spoken, -spoke*).

[iə – ɔː – ɔː]: *shear* (*shore, shorn*). Also weak.

[ei – ou – ou]: *break* (*broke, -en*).

[ɛə – ɔː – ɔː]: *bear* (*bore; borne, born*), *tear* (*tore, torn*), similarly *swear, wear*.

[e – ɔ – ɔ]: *forget* (*-got, -gotten*), similarly *beget, tread*; *get* (*got, got*).

[ʌ – ei – ʌ]: *come* (*came, come*).

[i – ʌ – ʌ]: *stick* (*stuck, stuck*).

---

[59] But *hove* is now in restricted use, and *got* is obligatory in British English; contrast *forgot*(*ten*).

[60] But see §232 note 56 above.

[61] **stecan* is the probable origin of ME *steken*, but is not in fact recorded in OE. I have added the asterisk in the text.

[62] The weak past forms (*sticked* etc.) appropriate to ME *stiken* survived into the 17th century, and much later in Scottish and dialectal use.

Class 5

OE type: *metan, mæt, mǣton, meten*.

§239 Most of the OE verbs of this class went over to Class 4 in
ME. A few, like *mete, bequeath*, became weak. The pret. *quoth*,
from OE *cweðan* 'say', has survived as an archaism. In the ModE
period the following belong here: *bid, give, sit; eat; lie* ('lie down');
see.

§240 *bid* (OE *biddan* 'ask') took over in ME the senses of OE
bēodan 'offer'; *forbid* essentially represents OE *forbēodan*, but was
re-formed in ME as *forbidden*. In the 16th century there are still one
or two forms belonging to OE (*for*)*bēodan*, such as the pret. (*for*)*bod*,
part. (*for*)*boden* etc. As a rule the pret. has had from the ME
period onwards the form *bad*, or, with analogical[63] lengthening,
bade; alongside it, the form *bid*, a new formation after the part.
bid(*den*), has existed since the 16th century. The part. originally had
the form *beden*, but this was in ME mostly re-formed as *bidden* under
the influence of the pres. Alongside *bidden, bid* developed; also, a
part. *bad*(*e*) is recorded in earlier ModE. The forms *bad*(*e*), *bid* of
the pret., and *bidden, bid* of the part. were formerly used without
differentiation of meaning. Nowadays in the pret. and part. *bid* is
virtually used only in the sense of 'offer, bid'; otherwise *bade* [bæd],[64]
bidden are the prevailing forms.

§241 *give* (ON *giva*)[65] has mostly the pret. *gave* with a long
vowel already in EModE; Part. *given*, rarely *give*.

§242 *sit* (OE *sittan, sæt, sǣton, seten*) had in earlier ModE *sat*,
sate in the pret. (with short and long vowel, ME *sat, saat*), beside a
not uncommon *sit* (after the part. *sitten*). The part. had the forms
sitten (a new formation on the pres. in place of ME *seten*), *sit*, or
sat, sate; the last two forms are already the only ones in Shakespeare.
Today *sat* [sæt] is the usual form in both pret. and part.; *sate* is
poetic.[66] The form *sitten* was in use up to the 19th century, though
mostly as a literary form.

The verb *spit* has joined this group in ModE; today pret. and part.
spat. Two verbs[67] have fallen together here: *spit* (OE *spittan*), pret.
and part. *spit*; and *spet* (OE *spǣtan*), pret. *spat, spet* (< OE *spǣtte*).

[63] See §232 note 56 above.
[64] Also [beid].
[65] O.Sw. *giva*, ODan. *give*.
[66] Now obsolete.
[67] Both originally weak verbs of the first conjugation.

§243 eat (OE *etan*, *ǽt*, *ǽton*, *eten*) had in the preterite in ME, alongside *ēt*, *at*, also *āt* with analogical vowel-lengthening.[68] In EModE only *at* (which was soon lost), *ate* (with a long vowel, the usual form) and *eat* (with [e]; perhaps a new formation after *lead* : *led* etc.)[69] are recorded with certainty. The PresE forms are *ate*, *eat*, usually pronounced [et] or [eit], less commonly [i:t].[70] The antiquity of PresE [i:t] is not known; perhaps it has arisen from *eat* through mistaken reading, or is a new formation after the part. *eaten*. Throughout the whole of the ModE period the part. had the forms still in use now: *eaten*, *eat*, *ate*; the latter two are in process of being abandoned, or have already been so.[71]

§244 lie (OE *licgan*, *læg*, *lǽgon*, *legen*). The pres. *lie* goes back to ME *līe* (a new formation replacing OE *licgan*, based on the 2nd, 3rd sing. pres. *ligest*, *ligeþ*); pret. *lay*, part. *layn* correspond to OE *læg*, *legen*. In earlier ModE the not uncommon part. *line* (*li'en* etc.) is due to the influence of the pres.

§245 see (OE *sēon*, *sēah*, *sēgon*, *gesegen* etc.).[72] The inflexion of this verb varied considerably in OE and ME. Already in EModE, however, *saw* (< ME *saw*, *saugh* < *seah*) was the prevailing form in the pret.; forms like *say*, *sy* (< ME *say*, *sy* < *seah*, *sēah*) occur only sporadically. *See* (probably a new formation after *seen*) is found rather more frequently. Already in ME the adj. *seen* (< OE *gesēne* 'visible') began to displace the old forms in the part.; only slight traces (*seyn* etc.) of the OE part. remain in ModE.

[68] See again §232 note 56 above. OE *ǽt*, though it would be normal, is not recorded; the actual form is *ǽt* (Anglian *ēt*) > ME *ę̄t*, *ẹ̄t*. But in ME a new pret. sing. *at* was formed on the analogy of regular verbs of this conjugation; it then became the basis of a new plural *aten*, in which occurred the lengthening which gave late ME *āt*.

[69] The spelling *eat* suggests that [et] descends from ME *ę̄t* with shortening; but the pattern of *lead* : *led* probably helped the shortened pronunciation to gain acceptance.

[70] Not now [i:t]. Ekwall is following Bradley in OED (1893), who gives this as a third alternative; but probably, as Ekwall suggests, it was a mistaken pronunciation used by persons who did not recognize *eat* as a written form of the pret. [et].

[71] Completely so now, except for *eat* in the nursery rhyme *Tom, Tom, the piper's son* (*The pig was eat . . .*).

[72] Ekwall's summary account of this very difficult verb is too brief, and implies mistaken views of the OE and ME development. He himself gives the pret. sing. as *sēah* in his list of principal parts; but OE *sēah* did not exist (though an early ME re-formation *sēh*, as if from OE *sē(a)h*, has to be assumed to account for late ME *sigh* 'saw' pret. sing.). The EModE pret. forms cited by Ekwall (*saw*, *say*, *sy*) in fact all derive from ME pret. pl. forms, not from the ME and OE pret. sing. forms, as he mostly implies. On the ME forms see Jordan, §63 and Anm. 1.

§246   PresE distribution:

[i – æ – i]: *bid* (*bade, bidden*, or *bid, bid*), *forbid* (*-bade, -bidden*).

[i – æ – æ]: *sit* (*sat, sat*), similarly *spit*.

[i – ei – i]: *give* (*gave, given*).

[iː – e, ei, iː – iː]: *eat* (*ate, eat*;[73] *eaten*).

[ai – ei – ei]: *lie* (*lay, lain*).

[iː – ɔː – iː]: *see* (*saw, seen*).

Class 6

OE type: *scacan, scōc, -on, scacen*.

§247   Several of the verbs belonging here became weak in ME (*ache, fare*, and others). The Scand. *take* joined this group in ME. In ModE *forsake, shake, take* usually have the regularly developed forms: pret. *shook* etc., part. *shaken* etc. In earlier ModE the forms *shook, forsook, took* were not uncommonly used as participles. *Take*, especially in poetry, had a participial form without *k* (*tane, ta'en*, etc.) which was already common in ME.

In a few verbs a strong participle was used in earlier ModE which is today mostly in adjectival use (such as *shapen, shaven*); *lade* still has part. *laden*; *gnaw*, part. *gnawn*,[74] *gnawed*.

§248   *stand* (OE *standan, stōd, -on, standen*). Only the part. has undergone any change in ModE. In EModE *standen* still existed alongside *stood* (recorded already in late ME) and the weak formation (*under*)*standed*. From the 17th century onwards *stood* is the dominant form; *understanded* occurs not uncommonly in quotations from the *Articles of Religion* of 1563.[75]

§249   (*a*)*wake*. OE (*on*)*wæcnan* (*wōc, -on, -wacen*) split in ME into the weak ME (*a*)*wakene* (ModE *awaken*) and the strong (*a*)*wake*. In ME the pret. of the latter for unexplained reasons[76] acquired an open instead of a close *ō*, which has given PresE [ou]. The pret. form had already displaced the old form of the part. in EModE; the latter has survived as the adj. *awake*. The verb (*a*)*wake* is often weak.

[73] On [iː] in the pret., see §243 note 70 above. The spelling *eat* for the pret. is old-fashioned.

[74] *gnawn* is now obsolete.

[75] I.e. the Thirty-Nine Articles.

[76] Clearly analogical, not phonetic; and the only verbs which could have provided a model for a pret. with *ǭ* in ME were those of the type (*a*)*rise*, pret. (*a*)*rose*, which has links in sense with (*a*)*woke*.

The weak *stave* 'break a hole in' has modelled itself on *wake*:[77] pret. and part. *stove, staved*.

§250   *draw* (OE *dragan, drōg, drōgon, dragen*). The pret. *drōg* (*drōh*), ME *drough* (*drow*) was displaced in ME by a new formation *drew*, which is usually explained as an analogical formation after the reduplicating verbs.[78] In the part. *drew* occurs sporadically in earlier ModE alongside the usual *drawn*.

§251   *slay* (OE *slēan, slōg -on, slǣgen, slagen*). Here also the old pret. (*slōg*, ME *slough, slow*) was displaced by a new formation *slew*. Already in ME the pres. *slay* had been re-formed after the part. *slayn*; the old form *slea* is still recorded in the 17th century.

§252   *wash* (OE *wascan*), *wax* (OE *weaxan*) are mostly weak in ModE. *Wash* still has the part. (*un*)*washen* in the Bible 1611. Forms like pret. *wox*, part. *waxen, woxen* from *wax* are to be found sporadically in EModE.

§253   PresE distribution:

[ei – u – ei]: *forsake* (*-sook, -saken*), similarly *shake, take*.

[æ – u – u]: *stand* (*stood, stood*).

[ei – ou – ou]: (*a*)*wake* (*-woke, -woke*),[79] similarly *stave*.

[ɔː – uː – ɔː]: *draw* (*drew, drawn*).

[ei – uː – ei]: *slay* (*slew, slain*).

REDUPLICATING VERBS

§254   Of the so-called reduplicating verbs several went out of use in the ME period or earlier, or adopted weak inflexions (e.g. *walk, dread, read, sleep, weep*). *Leap, let* show very occasional strong forms in the 16th century.

§255   *fall*. OE *f(e)allan, fēoll, -on, feallen* have given the expected *fall, fell, fallen* in PresE. OE *fēoll* became *fell* or *fill* in ME; the latter form is occasionally recorded in EModE. In earlier ModE *fell* occurred not infrequently in the part. (e.g. in Shakespeare).

§256   *hold* (OE *h(e)aldan, hēold, -on, h(e)alden*). The pret. *hēold* became ME *held* and *hild*, ModE *held*, and in the 16th century

---

[77] *break* would seem to be a more likely model on grounds of sense. According to OED *stove* (pret. and part.) is first recorded from the 18th century.

[78] This is probable, since the reduplicating verbs had become the most clearly marked type in which the infinitive and past part. had the same stem; also it was the class to which most verbs with stems ending in -*w* belonged.

[79] Also (*a*)*woken*, a difficult form, possibly modelled on *broken*; see further OED under *awake* and *wake*.

(rarely) *hild*. The old form of the part., *holden*, was in living use in the 17th century and still appears in legal language. The new formation *held* was already in use in the 16th century.

§257 *hang* has in ModE pret. and part. *hung* except in the sense 'execute by hanging' (in which case it is *hanged*).[80] The pres. *hang* derives from ME *hangen* (<OE *hōn, hēng, -on, hangen*, and OE *hangian*). The form *hung* (part.) has been borrowed from northern English; there the verb had the forms *hing* (<ON *hengia*), *hang*, *hung* (new formations on the model of *sing, sang, sung* etc.). The pret. *hung* was modelled on the part.

§258 *beat* (OE *bēatan, bēot, -on, bēaten*). We would expect the pret. [biːt] in EModE, but find only either [beːt], which is a new formation on the part. *beaten*, or [bet], probably an analogical formation on the model of *lead : led* etc. From [beːt] comes PresE *beat* [biːt]. In earlier ModE the part. had forms like *beaten, beat, bet(ten)*; today the form is *beaten*, but *beat* also occurs in the sense 'exhausted, defeated'.[81]

hew has the part. *hewn* beside *hewed* in ModE.

§259 *blow, grow* etc. OE *blāwan, blēow, -on, blāwen; grōwan, grēow, -on, grōwen* regularly gave ModE *blow, blew, blown; grow, grew, grown*. In earlier ModE weak forms like *blowed, growed*, are not at all uncommon; the part. *blowed* is still used as an imprecation.[82] *Crow* has pret. *crew, crowed*, part. *crowed*. *Mow, sow* have pret. *-ed*, part. *-n, -ed* (still pret. *mew, sew*, in the 17th century). *Snow* had pret. *snew* in the 17th century; *row* the part. *rown* in the 16th century (today *snowed, rowed*). The weak verbs *sew, show* often have analogically formed participles *sewn, shown*, both in use throughout the ModE period.

§260 PresE distribution:

[ɔː – e – ɔː]: *fall* (*fell, fallen*).

[ou – e – e]: *hold* (*held, held*).

[æ – ʌ – ʌ]: *hang* (*hung, hung*).

[iː – iː – iː]: *beat* (*beat; -en, beat*).

[juː – juː]: *hew* (*hewed; hewn, hewed*).

[ou – juː – ou]: *know* (*knew, known*).

---

[80] *hanged* is usually considered 'correct' in this sense, but only because of the archaism of the legal formula used in pronouncing sentence of death. In popular use *hung* is frequent and is historically justified. See further OED.

[81] Now only in the colloquial expression *dead beat*.

[82] Though a very mild one now.

[ou – uː – ou]: *blow* (*blew, blown*), similarly *grow, throw*; on *crow, mow, sow* see above.

2. WEAK VERBS

§261 The division of the weak verbs into three classes (I. *ja*-verbs, like *dēman, dēmde*; *nerian, nerede*; 2. *ō*-verbs, like *lōcian, lōcode*; 3. *ē*-verbs, like *secgan, sægde*) which is usually made in OE grammar, can no longer be maintained for the ME period, since the OE endings *-ode, -od* had become ME *-ede, -ed*, and the *i* in the present stem of Class 2 verbs had been early set aside by analogy, and thus the characteristic signs of this class were lost. From the standpoint of early ME[83] the weak verbs can be divided into two groups: (1) verbs making their pret. with *-ed*(*e*) (the larger group, which new formations and loanwords mostly follow), e.g. *loke*(*n*), *loked*(*e*); and (2) verbs which make their pret. with *-de, -te* (thus without an intermediate vowel), e.g. *hēre*(*n*), *herde*; *kēpe*(*n*), *kepte*.

In late ME the first *e* of the ending *-ed*(*e*) was usually syncopated[84] (the final *-e* had for the most part already become silent); *-de, -te* became *-d, -t*. The two groups did not fall together, however, since verbs of the second group showed in most cases special divergences, e.g. change of vowel etc. We can therefore divide the late ME and ModE weak verbs into (1) regular, and (2) irregular verbs, and these classes virtually coincide with the two (early) ME classes.

(a) Regular weak verbs

§262 The *e* of the ending *-ed* did not disappear in verbs with stems ending in *d, t*; the [d] resulting from *-ed* remained in verbs whose stems ended in a voiced sound, but became [t] when the stem ended in a voiceless one. This distribution is still current today. Examples: *nod, nodded* [nɔdid], *hate, -d* [heitid], *bathe, -d* [beiðd], *knock, -ed* [nɔkt].

---

[83] Ekwall is thinking here exclusively of East Midland and Northern dialects; his remarks do not apply to West Midland and Southern dialects, in which the OE conjugational system was much better preserved.

[84] The syncope of the ending *-ed* was less regular than Ekwall implies; 16th century observers, and even those of the earlier 17th century, often record the full forms (Dobson, §315). This accounts for the practice of poets—even dramatic poets—in freely using the full forms for metrical purposes, and also for the need, in printing poetry, to use special devices to indicate whether syncopated or full forms were intended by the poet.

I

As a rule, the ending of the pret. and part. are today written *-ed*. In earlier ModE (especially in the 17th and 18th centuries) the ending [d] was frequently indicated by *'d*, the ending [t] frequently by *t*; e.g. *glaz'd, hang'd, sav'd*; *blest, stopt, stretcht*. The orthographic rules current today (such as the alternation of single and double consonants: *nod, -ded*) were formed during the course of the ModE period.

(b) Irregular weak verbs

§263 Some differ from the regular ones only in having a long vowel in the pres. and a shortened one in the pret. What was originally only a quantitative distinction has, however, in the course of ModE become a qualitative one.

Of the OE type *dēman, dēmde*,[85] only *hear*, pret. *herd*, whence [hiə, hə:d], remained in late ME. *Herd* became *hard* in late ME by regular sound-change, and this was still in use in the 17th century; *herd* [herd] is due to the influence of the present.[86] A pret. with a long vowel (a new formation after *hear*) was not uncommon in earlier ModE.

Of the OE type *cēpan, cēpte*, only *keep* (: *kept*) remained in late ME and ModE, but this was joined at an early date by the originally strong *creep, leap, sleep, sweep, weep* (*crept, leapt, slept* etc.). *Leap* has also a pret. *leaped* [li:pt].

A new group was formed by verbs with stem ending in a vowel. From the ME period there belong in this category *flee* (pret. *fled*, ME *fledde, flede*; originally strong *fleih, fley* < OE *flēah*), *shoe* (*shod* < ME *schodde*, OE *scōde*). In ModE *say* : *said* [sed] has joined this group (cf. §16).

§264 The OE alternation between a mutated and an unmutated vowel in *sellan, s(e)alde* etc. has been retained in *sell, tell* (: *sold, told*). *Quell* (OE *cwellan, cw(e)alde*) has lost this variation.

§265 Some verbs in *l, m, n* add [t] instead of [d]: on the one hand *burn, dwell, learn, pen, smell, spill, spoil* etc., where the stem-vowel remains unchanged, on the other hand *deal, dream, feel, kneel, lean, mean* etc., which show a shortened vowel in the pret. This type developed in ME; in OE and EME these had preterites in *-de* or *-ode*,

---

[85] So Ekwall, but his argument requires the late OE form *demde* with shortened *e*. *Hear*, pret. *herd* goes back to late OE *hēran*, pret. *herde* (< earlier OE *hērde*).

[86] This is very doubtful, since the vowel of the pret. is self-evidently not that of the present. The late ME change of short *e* to *a* before *r*+cons. was not as regular as Ekwall assumes; *e* often remained as a variant beside *a*, as in this case. Cf. Dobson, §64 n. 3 and §65.

-*ede* (OE *dǣlan, dǣlde*; *leornian, leornode* etc.). Why [t] has replaced [d] here is not clear. In ModE regular forms (like [bɔːnd] beside [bɔːnt] etc.) are not uncommon; thus *dream* has pret. *dreamed* [driːmd], especially in a figurative sense, otherwise mostly *dreamt* [dremt].

§266 Several verbs with stems in [d, t] do not add a further [d, t]. The ending -*de* was in fact added in OE, but the [d] was absorbed by the [d, t] of the stem.

Of the OE type *blēdan, blēdde* there still survive *bleed, breed, feed, speed* with ME *ē̦*, EModE [iː]; *lead* with ME *ē̦*, EModE [eː]; *chide, hide* (pret. *bled, fed, sped, led, chid, hid*). *Chide, hide*, however, have mostly part. *chidden*,[87] *hidden*. The originally strong *read* (OE pret. *rǣdde* beside *rēd*) and *slide* have joined this group. On *ride* etc. in earlier ModE, cf. §213 f.

The OE type *mētan, mētte* has been less well preserved. Today only *meet* (*met*) of the old verbs of this class belongs here; in EModE *heat* 'make hot', *sweat* (still, e.g., in Cooper 1685), and *wet* still belonged here also.[88] In the ModE period *light* 'set fire to' and 'alight' (pret. since the 16th century *lit* beside *lighted*, ME *lighten*, pret. *lighte*), and the originally strong *shoot* (pret. *shot*) have been added to this group; on verbs like *bite* see §213 f.

Corresponding to the OE type *hreddan, hredde* there is PresE *rid*, pret. *rid* (but also *ridded*).[89] To this, by shortening of the vowel of the pres., have been added *shed* (still *sheed* : *shed* in EME), *shred* (OE *scrēadian*), *spread* (OE *sprǣdan, sprǣdde*). *Wed* (OE *weddian, weddode*) has sometimes *wed* in poetry besides the usual *wedded*.[90]

The OE type *cnyttan, cnytte* is still well represented. *Cut, knit, slit, split, thrust* (pret. *cut* etc.) have indeed belonged here since the OE period; in ME or later such verbs as *burst, cast, cost, hit, hurt, let, put* (pret. still *burst* etc.) have been added. *Knit*, however, has also the form *knitted*. In EModE there belonged here e.g. *lift* (pret. *lift* Bible 1611 etc.), *spit* (pret. *spit*; e.g. Shakespeare, Bible 1611; also *spet*, pret. *spet*), *start* (today *lifted* etc.).[91]

---

[87] Also *chid* (past part.) and *chided* in pret. and part.

[88] *heat* because it had a pret. [het] (still in colloquial use in the phrase *het up*); *sweat* and *wet* because the present stem was often pronounced with a long vowel (ME *ē̦*, [ɛː] > [eː]), the pret. with a short one.

[89] *ridded* is rare now. Note that Ekwall does not here say that *rid* comes from *hreddan*, but that it belongs to the same conjugational type. Cf. §66 and note 8.

[90] There is no characteristic poetic usage now; see the Introduction.

[91] Today the pret. and part. of *spit* are usually *spat*. This is properly the past stem of the otherwise obsolete verb *spete* (OE *spǣtan*, pret. *spǣtte* < earlier *spǣtte*); but in effect *spit* is now a strong verb of irregular type.

In this group also belong participles like *contract*, *infect*, *confiscate* etc. (<Lat. *contractus* etc.) with pres. *contract* etc. (pret. *-ed*), which were still in use in the 16th century.

§267 The OE type *sendan*, *sende* became early ME *sende(n)*, *sende*, whence soon (for reasons unclear) *sende(n)*, *sente* (ModE *send*, *sent*) developed. Like *send* there are nowadays *build*, *gild*; *bend*, *lend*, *rend*, *shend*, *spend*; *gird*. In EModE regularly constructed forms (*builded* etc.) were in use. These are today mostly poetic; a few forms of this kind, however, (like *blended*, *gilded*, *girded*) still occur also in prose.

§268 In the following cases more marked variations are shown by the pret. when compared with the pres.

[v, z] in the pres. > [f, s] in the pret.: *bereave* (*-reft*, *-reaved*; OE *rēafian*, *rēafode*), *cleave* (*cleft* etc.; cf. §220), *leave* (*left*, OE *lǣfan*, *lǣfde*), *lose* (*lost*; OE *losian*, *losode*),[92] *use* (pret. [juːst] 'was accustomed'; cf. §152). The change of [v, z] to [f, s] occurred in most cases in ME.

The OE type *tǣcean*, *tǣhte*; *sēcean*, *sōhte* has been well preserved. With pret. in *-aught* today there are only *teach* and the Fr. *catch*, which re-formed its pret. as *caught* in ME after *lachen*, *laughte*. The form *catched* was still used by good writers in the 18th century. *Reach* had frequently a pret. and part. *raught* till *c.* 1650 (almost the only form in Shakespeare). *Stretch* has pret. *stretched* in ModE. *Bring*, *buy*, *seek*, *beseech* have the regular pret. in *-ought*. *Work* always had the form *wrought* in the pret. and part. up to the 17th century; this form, which was frequently used even in its literal sense till towards the end of the 18th century, is today restricted to certain figurative senses (*it wrought a change* etc.).[93] *Owe* 'to own, owe', a pret. pres. vb in OE, had commonly a pret. *ought* till *c.* 1700 (today *owed*). The pret. *rought* from *reck* 'to care' was still in use in the 17th century.

Clothe has a pret. *clad* (or *clothed*).[94] *Clothe* represents OE

---

[92] Ekwall '*lose* < OE *lēosan*; *lost* < OE *losode*, *gelosod* from *losian*', thus repeating here his mistaken derivation of *lose*, while giving the correct derivation of *lost*. See §220 note 44.

[93] But note the adjectival use in *wrought iron*; and it is still possible to speak of a sculptor who 'wrought in brass'.

[94] But there is now a differentiation in usage: *clothed* is suitable for all contexts, while *clad* is literary and formal and normally used only in such semi-historical phrases as 'clad in rags', 'clad in knight's armour' etc.

clāðian; *clad* is from OE *clǣdde*, ME *cladde* belonging to OE *clǣðan*.

Make, *made*, go back to ME *make(n)*, *made* (OE *macian, macode*).

B. PERSONAL ENDINGS, ETC.

PRESENT

§269 The forms are: Pres. indic. 1st sing.: same as the pres. stem (ME *-e*); 2nd sing.: EModE *-(e)st*, rarely *-es*, today *-est* [-ist] (ME *-es(t)*); 3rd sing. EModE *-(e)th*, *-(e)s*, today *-(e)s*, pronounced [iz] after a sibilant, otherwise after voiced sounds [z], after voiceless ones [s] (ME *-eth, -es*); plural the same as the pres. stem, in EModE rarely *-en, -eth*[95] (ME *-e(n), -eth*); the pres. subjunctive, imp. and inf. the same as the pres. stem, except that in EModE the ending *-en* occurred rarely in the subjunctive pl. and inf. Pres. part. *-ing*.

§270 In the pres. indic. 3rd sing. *-eth* was the usual ending in the late ME standard language. The originally northern English ending *-s* is found only rarely. In the 16th century *-eth* greatly preponderates in prose, while in the drama and in poetry *-s* occurs frequently. Towards the end of the century *-s* appears frequently or predominantly even in some good prose-writers like Puttenham, Nash, Sidney. Probably *-s* was the ending current in colloquial speech in this period. In the 17th century *-s* became fully accepted in prose also. It is, e.g., used almost exclusively in Burton's *Anatomy of Melancholy* 1621, in Earle's *Micro-cosmography* 1628, and in Milton's prose. The forms *doth, hath* survived longer; they occur not infrequently up to the 18th century. In certain kinds of prose (as in legal language, and in religious prose modelled on the Bible of 1611, which is strongly dependent on the 1568 Bible-translation) the ending *-eth* remained long in use. In the 18th century the ending *-eth* was taken up again by poets, and it occurs not infrequently in later poetry. The ending is also to be found in archaising prose.

PRETERITE

§271 On the construction of the pret. and part., cf. §§209 ff. The

---

[95] There was also a pres. pl. in *-(e)s*, not uncommon, e.g., in the Shakespeare First Folio 1623.

pret. 2nd sing. has the ending -(e)st. However, forms without ending occur in the 16th century and later.

C. Anomalous Verbs

§272 Most are old pret.-presents whose pres. had originally been a pret. and had the appropriate endings.

§273 The substantive verb: *be*.

Pres. indic. 1st sing.: *am*; 2nd: *art*; 3rd: *is*. Pl. EModE *are, be*; PresE *are*. The form *be* (rarely *ben* < ME *bee(n)*, OE *bēoð*) was still in use in the 17th century but has now, except in the one expression *the powers that be* and in archaising style, been displaced by *are* (OE *earon*). In EModE *are* had an emphatic form with a long vowel, and an unemphatic form with a short one; PresE [aː] corresponds to EModE [ar]. The PresE forms are: [æm, (ə)m; aːt; iz, z; aː(r), ə(r)].

Pres. Subjunctive: *be*; 2nd sing. also *beest* in the 16th and 17th centuries; imper., inf.: *be*. Pres. part., *being*.

Pret. indic. 1st, 3rd sing.: *was*, today [wɔz, wəz]; 2nd sing.: EModE *were* (ME *were*), since the 16th century *wert, wast* (new formations modelled on *art*).[96] The two latter occur side by side through the whole of the ModE period. Pl. *were*, EModE [weːr][97] and [wer], the former being the emphatic, the latter the unemphatic form; [weːr] > [wɛə(r)]; [wer] > [wəː(r), wə(r)].[98] From the 16th to the 18th centuries *you was* was commonly used when addressing one person.

Pret. subjunctive, 1st, 3rd sing., pl.: *were*; 2nd sing.: EModE *were, wert*,[99] later *wert*.

Past part. *been* [biːn, bin].

§274 *can* has in ModE only the pres. *can* (2nd sing. *canst*), pret. *could* (2nd sing. *couldst*). Pret. *could* (ME *coude* for *coupe*, OE *cūðe*) owes its *l* to the influence of *should, would*; this *l* was occasionally pronounced up to the 18th century: [kuːld] beside [kuːd, kud].[1] PresE forms: [kæn, k(ə)n; kud, kəd].

---

[96] Not only on *art*, but on other such forms (*shalt, wilt*); but this *-t* ending was originally restricted to the present tense of these anomalous verbs. EModE also had *werst*, modelled on the regular -(e)st ending of normal verbs.

[97] [weːr] is more likely, since it is doubtful if late ME *ę̄* became [eː] before *r*. See Dobson, §203.

[98] Nowadays [wəː] is much commoner as an emphatic form than [wɛə].

[99] Also *werst*; see note 96 above.

[1] And other pronunciations; see Dobson, §4 (pp. 451–2).

§275 *dare* has pres. indic. 1st sing. and pl. *dare*, EModE also *dar* (< OE *dearr*; the long vowel in *dare* is exceptional);[2] 2nd sing. *darest*; 3rd sing. *dare*, *dares* (always *dares* when used with an object). Pret. *durst* (ME *durste* from OE *dorste* after the infin., OE *durran* etc.), and, since the 16th century, *dared*; this last form is now the current one. Occasional pret. *dare* has probably developed phonetically from sequences like *darednot*. Part. *durst* went out of use in the 17th century; PresE *dared*.[3]

§276 *do*: pret. *did*; part. *done*. The long vowel was frequently shortened in EModE; we find [duː, du; duːθ, duθ] etc.[4] PresE forms: *do* [duː, du, də], *does* [dʌz, dəz], *done* [dʌn].

§277 *go*: pret. *went*, really belonging to *wend*; part. *gone*, EModE [goːn], PresE [gɔn, gɔːn].[5]

§278 *have* lost its [v] in ME in the 2nd and 3rd sing. pres. indic., in the pret. and part., sometimes also in other forms (EModE still *ha'*, *a* for *have*). The form *have* occasionally had a long vowel in EModE.[6] PresE forms: *have* [hæv, (h)əv], *has* [hæz, (h)əz], *had* [hæd, (h)əd].

§279 *may* has in ModE pres. *may* (2nd sing. *-st* in place of OE *meaht, miht*); pret. *might* (OE *mihte*), EModE also *mought* (ME *moghte*). The pres. pl. still occasionally had the form *mowe* (OE *mugon*) in EModE.

§280 *must* is undeclined in ModE. *Must* is really the pret. of the archaic ModE *mote* (OE *mōt*, pret. *mōste*).

§281 *need*, in OE and ME a regularly inflected weak verb (OE *nēodian*, ME *nēden*), has since the 16th century *need* in the 3rd pres. sing. alongside *needs*. Pret. *need* also occurs occasionally from the 18th century on.[7]

§282 *ought* is undeclined in ModE apart from the 2nd pers. *ought(e)st*. *Ought* represents OE *āhte*, pret. of *āgan*, whence *owe* (§268).

§283 *shall* has in ModE 1st, 3rd pres. sing. and pl. *shall*, 2nd sing.

---

[2] ME *dar* was made the basis of new inflected forms (2nd sing. *daryst*, later *darest*; infin. and pres. pl. **dare(n)*) in which open-syllable lengthening could occur; in late ME and EModE the lengthened vowel would than have been generalized.

[3] *dare* has been gradually becoming a regular verb, but the process is not yet complete.

[4] After *c.* 1640 *doth* was [dʌθ] < earlier [duθ].

[5] [gɔn] is now much commoner than [gɔːn].

[6] So also *hast, hath*.

[7] Alongside regular *needed*.

shalt, pret. *should* (2nd sing. -*st*). *Should* (<OE *sculde* in place of
OE *scolde* after the pres. pl. OE *sculon*, inf. *sculan*) varied in EModE
like *could* between forms with and without *l* [ʃuːld, ʃuːd, ʃud].[8] The
loss of [l] may be due to the influence of *could*, or may be due to
weak stress. The [uː] is probably due to the influence of *could*.[9]
PresE forms: [ʃæl, ʃ(ə)l; ʃud, ʃəd].

§284   *will* has in ModE mostly the pres. *will*, 2nd sing. *wilt*, pret.
would. Beside *will* (*wilt*) from ME *wille* etc. there occur in EModE
forms with *o*, *u* (cf. ME *wolle*, *wole* etc., which are to be explained
as due to the influence of *w*[10] or of the pret. *wolde*); cf. *woo't* = *wilt*
in Shakespeare. On the shortened forms [l, lt] such as *I'll* etc. recorded since the 16th century, cf. §134. *Would* (ME *wulde*, *wolde*,
OE *wolde*) has developed like *should*.[11] PresE forms: [wil, l; wud,
wəd, (ə)d].

§285   *wot* (OE *witan*, pres. *wāt*, pret. *wiste*) was already in EModE
little used except in the expression *God wot* and in the inf. (*to*) *wit*.
Pres. pl. *wit*, pret. *wist* (<OE *witon*, *wiste*) and new formations like
wots (3rd sing. pres.), *wotting* (pres. part.) are also occasionally
recorded in EModE.

Negative Forms

§286   Forms of auxiliary verbs are often contracted into mono-
syllabic forms with the particle *not*. In such cases the stem-vowel has
often undergone marked changes.

The following have an *a*-vowel: *a'n't* (*an't*, later *arn't*, *aren't*)
for *am* (*are*, *is*) *not*, today only for *are not*;[12] *can't* (*cannot*); *han't*
for *have* (*has*) *not* (now obsolete); *shan't* for *shall not*. *a'n't* probably
derives from *am* (*are*) *not* and was later used also for *is not*. The
PresE pronunciation is [aː], thus [kaːnt, ʃaːnt] etc.; the ancestor of
this pronunciation is given by Lediard 1725.[13]

An *i*-vowel is found in *in't*, now out of use; PresE [iznt]. Cf.
i'not Ben Jonson. Pronunciation: [iːnt, int].

An *o*-vowel occurs in *don't* for *do not*, earlier often for *does not*

---

[8] And other pronunciations; cf. Dobson, §4 (pp. 456–7).

[9] But emphatic late OE *scōlde* is a more obvious and more likely source.

[10] This is much more likely; spellings with *u* are earlier than, and continue
beside, those with *o*, and indicate that the vowel was [u] by rounding of *i* after *w*.

[11] For the EModE pronunciations see Dobson, §4 (pp. 462–3).

[12] In questions, [aːnt ai] for *am not I* is in regular use.

[13] For a detailed explanation of the [aː] in *can't*, *aren't*, see Dobson, §238.

also; cf. *he do'not* Ben Jonson; *won't* for *will not* (really for *wull not* or *wol not*).[14] PresE pronunciation [dount, wount], earlier [doːnt woːnt] in Lediard 1725.

Some of the contracted forms are recorded from the 16th century onwards (e.g. *can't, won't*). There are great difficulties in the way of explaining these forms. An emphatic lengthening has been suggested (cf. *leetle* for *little* as a result of strong emphasis). However this does not, e.g., explain the loss of [z] in *i'nt* etc. [ou] in *don't* is remarkable.[15]

---

[14] Dobson (§95 n.) explains *won't* as due to late ME *ou* < *ŭ* + *l*; see also §425 n. 4.
[15] Because of the difference from the vowel of *do*; but there is evidence of a 17th century [doː], probably from a ME weak form with short *o* (Dobson, §4, p. 452), and this could well explain *don't*, recorded from only a little later.

K

WORD-LIST

Ekwall notes that the word-list 'makes no claim to completeness, but contains a (fairly copious) selection chiefly of the words dealt with in the phonology. Certain frequently occurring prefixes and suffixes (such as *con-* in *concur*, *-age* in *cottage*) have also been included'.

I have thought it best to preserve the character of this selection as of the rest of the work. I have, however, altered the page-references to paragraph-references in the belief that this will make consultation of the text easier and quicker. Also, I have in some cases added a few distinguishing labels (such as 'sb.', 'vb') to make clearer which word is being referred to, as well as correcting a sprinkling of errors, and have added extra references where I have noticed these to be incomplete. A few minor typographical changes have also been made.

a, an, 165, 197
-a (as in *idea*), 109, 132
absolute, 65
absolve, 105, 154
abuse, 146
acacia, 155
acceptable, 10
access, -ary, 10
accomplish, 100
accoutre, 83
-ace (as in *palace*), 111
ache, 178
acknowledge, 178
acorn, 22
actual, 171
-ade (as in *charade*), 9
adventure, 171
aeroplane, 30
afford, 83, 142
again, -st, 21, 114
-age (as in *cottage*), 111
ajar, 158
-al (as in *final*), 108
album, 35
alcohol, 104
Alexander, 106, 150
Alfred, 35
allhallows, 7
almanack, 44, 127
almighty, 6, 44, 127
almond, 44, 175
almoner, 44
almost, 44, 127
alms, 44, 127
Alnwick, 127

Alps, 35
altitude, 35
always, 112
amber, 38
ambrosia, 148, 155
ambsace, 38, 168
ambush, 11
amen, 12, 13
among, 96; -st, 181
amour, 86
-an (as in *ocean*), 108
ancestor, 35
anchovy, 10
ancient, 40
and, 175
angel, 39, 160
anger, 181; angry, 181
anguish, 35, 157, 181
anon, 16
answer, 6, 47, 134, 144
ant, 47
-ant (as in *pleasant*), 108
anthem, 170
Anthony, 170
anxiety, 105, 150
any, 26
apothecary, 170
appear, 52, 58
appreciate, 119
apron, 118
arch-, 178; bishop, 13, 14, 178
are, 16, 273; aren't, 286
argument, 106
artisan, 45
as, 145

ask, 43; asked, 178
-asm (as in *enthusiasm*), 153
aspect, 10, 46
ass, 46
assault, 35, 128
assignation, assignee, 182
associate, 155; association, 119, 155
asthma, 170
asylum, 148
-ate (as in *private*), 111
august (adj.), 9
aunt, 43, 45
Australia, 105
authentic, 170
author, 170
autocrat, 104
avalanche, 45
ay, 71

backgammon, 7
balm, 42, 44, 128
banquet, 135
basis, 148
bath, 43, 46, 188; Bath, 142
bathe, 28, 29, 141, 142
be, 58, 59, 273
be- (as in *become*), 105
bear, 56, 234, 238
beard, 17, 57
Beatrice, 116
Beau-, 51, 61
beauty, 61
because, 16
been, 273
behove, 87
belch, 158
belief, 138
bellows, 189
bench, 158
beneath, 51, 142
bequeath, 142
Berkshire, 48
Berlin, 13, 14
besom, 22
betroth, 142
bier, 52
bilge, 160
biography, 105
biscuit, 112
blackguard, 7, 178
Blackheath, 7
blancmange, 45
blasphemous, 10

blood, 16
blue, 63, 65
boa, 78
board, 17, 83, 85
boatswain, 112, 134, 177
boil (sb.), 92, 93; (vb), 94
Bolingbroke, 100
bomb, bombast, 100
bonfire, 21
book, 16
booth, 142
born(e), 81, 232, 234, 238
borough, 109
both, 142
bough, 101, 163
bought, 163
bound (adj.), 176
bouquet, 105, 135
bow (sb.), 88; (vb.) 101
bowl, 88, 91
boy, 92, 93, 94
brazier, 155
bread, 16
break, 54, 238; -fast, 21, 108
breathe, 52
breeches, 19
briar, 69
bridegroom, 132
brief, 58
bristle, 172
Bristol, 128
Britain, 112
broad, 80
brook (sb.), 16; (vb) 103
brought, 88, 90, 163
build, 17
bulb, 98
bulk, 98
bull, bullet, 98
buoy, 92, 94, 95
burden, 142
bury, 48, 50
bush, 98
bushel, 96, 98, 110
business, 116; busy, 144
Byron, 118

cabbage, 111, 158
Caesar, 148
Caithness, 170
Caius College, 33
Calais, 112
calf, 42, 44, 188

half, 42, 43, 44, 45, 127; -penny, 41, 116, 137
hallo, 13
halm, 44
-ham (as in *Pelham*), 165, 181
Hampton, 167
handkerchief, 110, 122, 175
handsome, 144, 175
han't, 286
harbinger, 124
harlequin, 135
haunt, 35, 45
have, 16, 165, 278
he, 58, 165, 198, 200
head, 16
heal, 51; -th, 142
hear, 52, 263; -d, 263; see also 261
hearken, 25
heart, 25
hearth, 25
heaven, 22
heavy, 22
heifer, 163
height, 34
heir, 166
her, 165, 200, 203
herald, 48, 128
herb, 82, 166
here, 58, 60; -after, 7
hereditary, 165
hideous, 119, 174
him, 165, 198, 200
hind 'servant', 176
his, 145, 165, 202, 203
historical, 165
hoard, 17
hock, 163
hoise, hoist, 92, 93
Holborn, 127
holiday, 72
holy, 22
honest, honour, 166
-hood (as in *livelihood*), 165
horizon, 9
hospital, 75, 166
hot, 16
hotel, 105
hough, 163
hour, 101, 120, 130, 166
house, 101, 144, 145, 188; -wife, 110, 134
hoy, 92, 95
human, 166

humble, 96, 166, 168
Humphrey, 166
hundred, 110
hurrah, 13
husband, 21
hussar, 154
huzzy, 134, 137, 144

I, 198, 200
-ial (as in *bestial*), 155, 171
iamb, 168
-ian (as in *Christian*), 119, 171
-ible (as in *possible*), 106
-ice (as in *surplice*), 110
idea, 9, 60, 105, 132
-ier (as in *courtier*), 119, 171
if, 137
-il, -ile (as in *pupil, missile*), 110
impostor, 9, 75
impregnable, 182
-in (as in *cousin*), 110
in- (as in *increase*), 122
income, 104
India, 132, 174; -ian, 119, 174
indict, 178
individual, 174
-ine (as in *columbine*), 110
infantry, 10
-ing (as in *morning*), 125
insular, 156
insult, 104
in't, 286
interpolate, 11
interstice, 10
-ion (as in *nation*), 108, 119, 155, 162, 171
-ious (as in *glorious*), 119
Ipswich, 134, 158
iron, 118
is, 145, 152, 273
island, 69
-ism, 153
issue, 109, 156, 157
it, 165, 198, 200
italics, 105
-ite (as in *finite*), 110
-ity (as in *unity*), 106

jamb, 38
jaundice, 35, 45
jaunt, 45; -y, 45, 127
jeopardy, 48
jewel, 63
joist, 92, 93

key, 33
kiln, 123
kindred, 110
know, 178, 260; -ledge, 22, 158

lamb, 168
landlady, 175
language, 135, 181
languid, languor, 135
lapel, 9
lass, 46
lath, 188
Latham, 142
latitude, 112, 171
laudanum, 23
laugh, 35, 43, 46
launch, 45
lawn, 175
lead (vb), 16, 266
learn, 17, 58, 265
lease, 146
Leicester, 116
length, 181
lens, 148
Leominster, 123
Leonard, 48
Lesbian, 153
-less, -let (as in *useless, violet*), 110
lettuce, 112
levee, 10
Lewisham, 157
lieutenant, 138
limb, 168
limetree, 122
Lincoln, 127
linger, 66, 67
liquid, liquor, 135
Lisbon, 146
listen, 172
literature, 171
loll, 88
London, 175
long, 72, 73, 125, 181; -er, -est, 181; -ish, 181
loose, 83, 145
lose, 220, 268
louse, 144, 145; lousy, 145
love, 83
lunatic, 65
luxury, luxurious, 156

machine, 58
madam, 47

mail, 32
maintain, 105
mankind, 7
many, 26
Marlborough, 131
marquis, 135
Mars, 148
mason, 146
masquerade, 135
mass, 46
mastiff, 46
maulstick, 36
maunder, maundy, 45
me, 58, 198, 200
measure, 23, 156, 159
memoir, 10
merchant, 48
Mesmer, 153
messenger, 106, 124
midden, 125
mid stream, 13
mien, 58
mine (pron.), 201, 203
minute (sb.), 112
mis- (as in *misdeed*), 6
mischief, 110; mischievous, 10
miser, 148
mister, mistress, 105
mistletoe, 153
Moll, 88
-monger, 96
months, 140
moor, 83, 85, 86; Moor, 83
mortgage, 172
mote (vb), 87
mother, 22, 142
mould, 88
moult, 128
mountain, 112
mourn, 17, 101, 103
mouse, 145
-mouth (as in *Portsmouth*), 142
move, 83
murder, 142
muscle, 178
museum, 105, 154
muslin, 153
my, 201, 203; -lady, -lord, 201; -self, 7

nap, 74
naphtha, 137
near, 52
neither, 33, 34

pretext, 10
pretty, 66
prism, 153
professor, 9, 105
pronunciation, 155
proof, 83, 138
prosecute, 11
prosody, 148
prow, prowl, 91
psalm, 44, 167; -ist, -ody, 44
psalter, 167
ptisan, 167
puck, 103
pulp, 98
purpose, 149

quadrant, quadrate, 75
quaff, 27
quaint, 133
quality, quantity, 27
quay, 33
quinsy, 149
quoit, 135
quote, quotidian, 135

rack 'arrack', 114; 'rack' (sb.), 49
raisin, 33, 110
Ralph, 28
raspberry, 153, 167
rather, 47
re- (as in *recover* 'cover again'), 104,
    (as in *retain*), 105
read, 52, 266
realm, 128
reason, 51, 53, 146
receipt, 33
reck, 178
recognize, 182
recoil, 92
record, 104
regular, 106
resemble, 154
resent, 154
reserve, 147
reservoir, 10, 36
residue, 174
resource, 147
resume, 147
retinue, 10
reveille, 49
revolt, 88
revolution, 65
rhythm, 121, 140

ribband, 176
rid, 66, 266
righteous, 171
rise, 144, 209, 213, 217
roast beef, 13, 172
roe (of a fish), 89
roister, 92
Rome, 83
room, 83, 103
rouge, 159
rough, 163
round (vb), 176
rouse, 144
rowlock, 81
rude, 63, 64

sack (the wine), 49
sage (the herb), 28
said, 16, 263; see also 261
Saint, 105, 172
St Clair, St John, 105
salmon, 25, 26, 128
salt, 20, 35
salvation, 44
salve, 42, 44, 127
sample, 35, 45
sauce, 36
saunter, 35
sausage, 23, 36, 146
savage, 25
save, 28
says, 16
scalp, 44, 127
scarce, 18, 28, 30
scene, 51
schedule, 178
schism, 121, 153, 178
scissors, 146
scream, 54
scroll, 88
search, 48, 51, 57
sedan, 9
seignior, 182
sergeant, 25
servant, serve, 48
seven, 22; -night, 110, 138
sew, 61, 88, 259
sewer, 61, 86
Shakespeare, 21
shall, 35, 283; shalt, 127, 283
shalm, 44
shan't, 127, 286
she, 198, 200